The Tunisian Crochet Handbook

The Tunisian Crochet Handbook

A BEGINNER'S GUIDE

TONI LIPSEY

PHOTOGRAPHY BY ALLIE LEHMAN

ABRAMS ■ NEW YORK

123

85

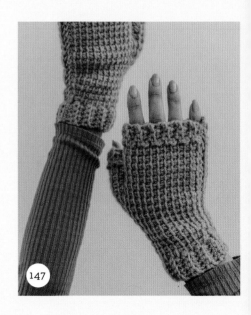

147

To my Mommy Salami, *from your* Toni Macaroni

81

77

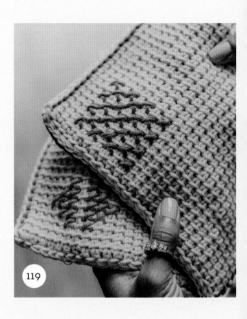

119

Contents

Welcome

I held my first crochet hook at just thirteen years old. After exhausting all of my entertainment options over what felt like an excruciatingly long summer break, I turned to my multitalented mother for some ideas. Gwennie handed me what I came to learn was a granny square and told me to "keep going." The rest of the summer was a flurry of yarn. In my eyes, I'd made the next artistic masterpiece. In reality, I'd made a hideously wonky camouflage blanket that would promptly be donated to the local thrift store.

That initial encounter with yarn and the sense of accomplishment I felt took root in my creative spirit and blossomed in my adult life. My short-lived positions in nonprofit organizations and human resources work were eclipsed by my unwavering attraction to hooks and string. After selling my wares at countless craft markets, TL Yarn Crafts was born and I dove into it full time. I now get the honor of spending my days with bottomless cups of coffee and endless shelves of beautiful fiber. I split my time between designing modern patterns that elevate the crochet aesthetic and sharing my maker knowledge through instructional blog posts, technique videos, and full project classes.

My interest in Tunisian crochet was first piqued during a chance encounter at a yarn convention. I turned a corner and stumbled upon a woman crocheting with what looked like a massive knitting needle. She indulged my request to give it a try and told me all about Tunisian crochet history and this interesting yarn craft style. Tunisian crochet has always had an air of mystery, likely attributed to the fact that craft historians still cannot pinpoint its true origin. Add that Tunisian crochet has had many different names over the centuries (afghan crochet, shepherd's knitting, and Princess Frederick William stitch, among others), and it's easy to see why Tunisian crochet is often misunderstood.

No matter the enigmatic history, one cannot deny the beauty and versatility of Tunisian crochet. Early stitchers embraced the thick, dense fabric created by this crochet style, using the stitches to make warm blankets and heavy sweaters. As time and techniques progressed, lacier fabrics came to life, challenging preconceived notions of what Tunisian crochet could do. Presently, clever designers are pushing the boundaries of Tunisian and sharing its wonders with a whole new audience.

The Tunisian Crochet Handbook was written to lay the foundation for your inevitable exploration of this addictive yarn craft and inspire your first (or next!) Tunisian crochet project. By understanding the various tools, techniques, and stitches, you are building an invaluable tool kit of knowledge that will prepare you for any pattern you take on. Processes that took me years to master are distilled into easily digestible tutorials with myriad applications.

The latter half of this book, which houses twenty distinctly modern patterns, is where you can put your new knowledge to the test. Meander through classic housewares, chic wearables, and timeless accessories, all while experimenting with fibers not often associated with crochet. Watch your confidence soar as you complete project after satisfying project, reinforcing the skills learned in previous sections.

What started as a cure for my teenage boredom has morphed into a lifelong passion, a thriving maker community, and a gratifying career. *The Tunisian Crochet Handbook* stands as the physical embodiment of the craft that rekindled my affection for all things crochet. My singular desire in writing this guide is to give you the resources and encouragement needed to master this unique craft. I hope this book serves as a valuable reference on your personal maker journey. Stitch by stitch and row by row, I know that you too will fall in love with Tunisian crochet. Happy crocheting!

xo,
Toni L.

ESSENTIALS

Tools + Materials

HOOK TYPES

Tunisian crochet has a unique construction, setting it apart from both traditional crochet and knitting. The forward pass of Tunisian involves collecting loops across the width of your fabric. The potential width of your project is limited by the length of your hook. Adjust your hook based on your current project.

Fixed Tunisian Hook (1)

Typically made of wood or aluminum, fixed Tunisian hooks are about 12 inches (30.5 cm) long with a crochet hook head on one end and a stopper on the other end. These are great hooks to practice with and are often available in inexpensive sets.

Crochet Hook (2)

Regular crochet hooks come in handy when working Tunisian crochet. Narrow projects like ear warmers and coasters can be completed without using a special hook. Since you will need to accumulate loops on the hook, look for a straight hook without any adornments or shaping in the handle. You may also want to use a traditional crochet hook for adding borders.

Double-Ended Crochet Hook (3)

Work Tunisian crochet in the round using a double-ended hook. These hooks vary in length but accomplish the same thing. When shopping for double-ended hooks, be sure to purchase one where the hook heads on either side are the same size. You can also use interchangeable crochet hooks as double-ended hooks. Connect two hooks of the same size to either end of a cable for a custom double-ended hook.

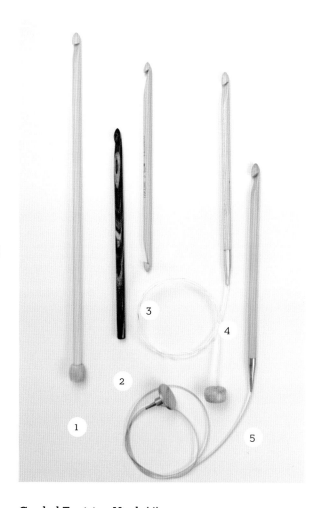

Corded Tunisian Hook (4)

Corded Tunisian hooks have a crochet hook head on one end and a cable fastened to the tapered opposite end of the hook. The longer the cord, the more loops you can collect during the forward pass, opening your possibilities to items like afghans and garments. Keep an eye on the connection between the cable and the hook—low-quality hooks are often connected to their cables with glue, which can detach over time.

Interchangeable Tunisian Hook (5)

Like corded Tunisian hooks, interchangeable hooks have a crochet hook head at one end, but the other end has been altered to allow the user to swap out flexible cables of varying lengths. A stopper is affixed to the other end of the cable to prevent loops from falling off. Most Tunisian crochet hook sets also come with extenders to make cables even longer.

HOOK MATERIALS

With the recent popularity of the craft, Tunisian crochet hooks and hook sets are easier to find in a variety of materials. Choosing the right hook is unique to every crocheter. Practice with each material type mentioned to determine the best fit for you.

Metal (1)

Metal hooks are strong and often have the most consistency from hook to hook. For Tunisian crochet, it's likely you'll only find metal hooks that are fixed. While you are limited in the types of projects you can make with these hooks, you can rest assured that metal hooks will stand the test of time.

Plastic (2)

Plastic hooks are lightweight and typically inexpensive. They play well with just about any kind of yarn and offer a medium, even tension. Beware of plastic-on-plastic friction when using acrylic yarns with plastic hooks—the repeated motion can cause a vibration that is irritating to those with sensitive joints.

Wood and Bamboo (3)

Natural fibers like wood and bamboo are the best choice for hand health when it comes to Tunisian crochet. It also helps that you can find fixed, corded, and interchangeable Tunisian crochet hooks in wood and bamboo while other options are typically limited.

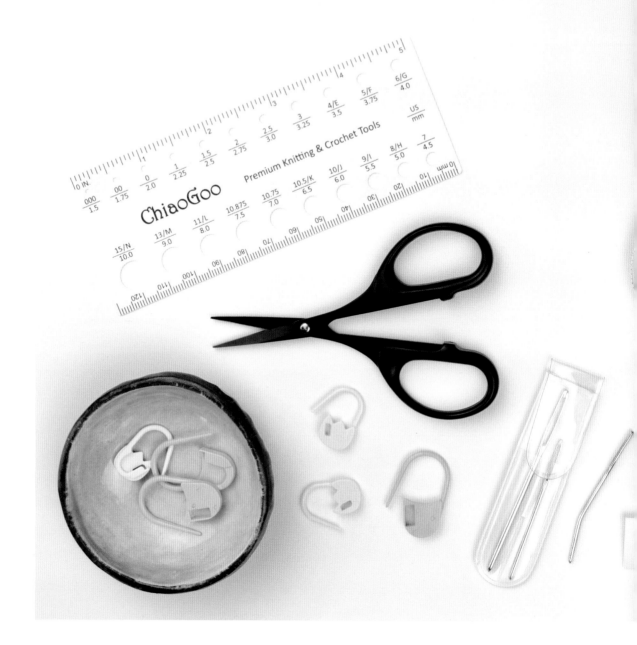

NOTIONS

Aside from hooks, there will be plenty of odds and ends to keep your project bag full. Notions are the extras that make the crochet process fun, productive, and accurate. Keep these supplies close so you always have them handy, regardless of the project.

Locking Stitch Markers

Stitch markers are useful in so many ways. Mark your stitches to help you keep count of rows, identify special stitches in the pattern, and even hold on to your live loop when you need to store your projects. There are designated locking stitch markers that you can find at craft stores, but you can also use a bobby pin, paper clip, or even a scrap piece of yarn as a stitch marker.

Tape Measure

A crafter's staple, the tape measure is vital for keeping track of measurements within your project.

Ruler

A rigid ruler is especially helpful for measuring gauge (more on that later). Getting accurate gauge is super important, so I always reach for a ruler over a tape measure in this instance.

Hook and Stitch Gauge

A needle gauge is a helpful multitasker if you don't have a ruler handy. Most will have a 2-inch (5-cm) or 4-inch (10-cm) ruler on them. You'll also find several holes in them that correspond to standard crochet hook sizes. If the size has been rubbed off your hooks, try placing them in different holes to determine each hook's size.

Tapestry Needle

Metal and plastic tapestry needles (aka yarn needles) are great for weaving in ends, adding embroidery, and affixing tassels. If you don't have one handy, try a crochet hook instead.

Blocking Supplies

Rustproof pins, foam mats (aka blocking boards), wool wash, and garment steamers help put the finishing touches on your projects. Tunisian crochet is particularly susceptible to curling, and blocking at the end will produce an even, flat fabric.

Scissors

Small embroidery scissors are a great choice for making your project mobile. Also, keep a pair of large, sharp scissors at home for cutting fringe and trimming pom-poms.

Reading a Pattern

Reading Tunisian crochet patterns can seem a little tricky when you're just starting out. At first glance, patterns are just a collection of text, abbreviations, and punctuation. Once you get a handle on what all of these purposefully placed elements mean, the pattern will reveal itself. Like learning a new language, reading these patterns will get easier with practice.

The first step is reading the pattern through, from beginning to end. The construction may not make total sense in the beginning, but this memory may serve you well once your hooks start going.

Every Tunisian crochet designer has a personal pattern-writing style. But to make patterns mostly universal, we all use a standard set of pattern elements. Look out for the following in most Tunisian crochet patterns:

YARN

Crochet designers list the yarn used in the pattern, including the yarn brand, attributes, colors, and the amount of yarn used for each color where applicable. The assumption is that using the exact yarn (and other materials) listed while meeting that pattern gauge will give you an exact replica of the original sample. If you plan to substitute for a different yarn, be sure to check and adjust your gauge.

TOOLS AND NOTIONS

Patterns will include the hook(s) used, as well as any additional notions and supplies. Be sure to gather these supplies early in the project, so you won't be caught without them when you need them.

SIZE

The size section will give you the dimensions for the finished project. This can vary based on the item being made. A project like a washcloth may only offer the length and width, but a project like a cardigan will have dimensions for each of the sizes offered. When it comes to garments, look for terms like "finished bust" or "sized to fit" to determine which size to make for yourself.

GAUGE

Gauge is the number of stitches and rows it takes to reach a certain measurement, typically about 4 inches (10 cm) square. Matching the designer's gauge will ensure you get the correct finished dimensions and use the recommended amount of yarn. Gauge is less important for a blanket or scarf, but it is vital for wearables. Skip ahead to the Gauge section (page 17) for more on this topic.

SHORTHAND

To make patterns even easier to read, an individual stitch repeat may be written in shorthand. For example,

Instead of writing: **Tss each of the next 6 stitches**
A designer may write: **Tss 6**.

PUNCTUATION

Another aspect of pattern writing is the use of asterisks *, brackets [ ], and parentheses ( ). Each of these elements is used as a form of shorthand within the pattern, similar to how abbreviations are used.

Asterisk—An asterisk begins a set of instructions that will be repeated (abbreviated "rep"). That set of instructions is then followed by a semicolon, a comma, or another asterisk to indicate the end of the repeated instructions. The information after the semicolon, comma, or asterisk will tell you how many times to repeat those instructions.

For example:

> *yo, sk 1, tss next st; rep from * to end of row.
>
> The instructions between the * and the ; will be repeated as many times as possible until the row is complete.

Brackets and Parentheses—These punctuation marks can be found in many places throughout a pattern, and their meaning mainly depends on the context in which they are used. While parentheses are found most often in patterns, they can be used interchangeably or in conjunction with brackets.

To indicate repeats:

> Tss 5, [(Tss 1, inc) 3 times, tss 1] 4 times, Lts, RetP.
>
> The instructions within the parentheses are repeated three times. Then complete the remaining instructions within the brackets. Finally, repeat the whole set of bracketed instructions three more times (four times total).

To clarify stitch counts:

> **ROW 2:** Tss 1, inc, tss 19, inc, tss 1, Lts, RetP. (27 tss)
>
> The number in parentheses at the end of the row indicates the total number of stitches in that row. This will only be present if the stitch count of the current row is different from the stitch count of the previous row.

To identify sizes:

> Sizes: S/M (L/XL, 2XL/3XL)
>
> Bust: 54 (60, 66)" [137 (152, 168.5) cm]
>
> Length: 27 (28, 29)" [69 (71, 74) cm]
>
> Garment patterns with multiple sizes will use parentheses to separate measurements and stitch counts into their respective sizes. To help keep your pattern organized, use a highlighter to highlight the specific instructions and stitch counts for the size you are making.

To clarify instructions:

> **ROW 70:** Tss2tog over next 2 sts, tss2tog over next st and last st (insert hook under both loops of last st as for Lts), RetP.
>
> The text within the parentheses serves to specify how to insert the hook into the last stitch, thus preemptively answering that question for the maker.

ABBREVIATIONS

Tunisian crochet abbreviations include some traditional crochet terms like "ch" for chain, but the majority of Tunisian crochet abbreviations are exclusive to the craft. The abbreviations are a shorthand way of giving instruction within the pattern.

As you become more familiar with reading patterns, most abbreviations will become like second nature. There's no need to memorize all of the abbreviations, though. Most individually sold patterns will include a helpful key of abbreviations near the very beginning or very end of the pattern.

Here is a list of many common Tunisian crochet terms for stitches and actions, some terms that are specific to traditional crochet, and a few special terms you will see within *The Tunisian Crochet Handbook*:

BLO	back loop only
Cc	change color
Ch	chain
Dec	decrease
Etss	extended Tunisian simple stitch
FLO	front loop only
FwdP	forward pass
Inc	increase
Lts	Last Tunisian stitch
Rep	repeat
RetP	return pass
Reverse Sc	reverse single crochet
RS	right side
Sc	single crochet
Sk	skip
Sl st	slip stitch
St(s)	stitch(es)
Tdc	Tunisian double crochet
Tfs	Tunisian full stitch
Tks	Tunisian knit stitch
Tps	Tunisian purl stitch
Trs	Tunisian reverse stitch
Tss	Tunisian simple stitch
Tss2tog	Tunisian simple stitch 2 together (decrease made)
Tss3tog	Tunisian simple stitch 3 together (decrease made)
WS	wrong side
Yo	yarn over

Gauge

Let's say you give two crocheters the same yarn and hook and ask them to make a square of Tunisian simple stitch that is twenty stitches wide and twenty rows long. It is likely that the finished swatches will be two different sizes although they were both done correctly. This difference is a result of tension and is a product of how tightly or loosely each person crochets.

Gauge is the idea that we can adjust our tension to meet a certain number of stitches and rows for a given measurement. To keep things standard, you will typically find gauge measured over a 4-inch by 4-inch (10-cm by 10-cm) square of crocheted fabric. Checking your gauge at the start of a project is crucial to ensure that your finished dimensions are correct and that you use the recommended amount of yarn.

It is often suggested that gauge does not matter for projects with variable dimensions like washcloths or scarves. I tend to disagree. While you can easily adjust the number of stitches or rows in a project to get the finished size you want, gauge also references the density of a project, which impacts the drape and potential usefulness of a project.

For example, if you are hoping to make a fabric with a tight weave to use as a hot pad but you have loose tension, the resulting fabric may be too airy and unusable for the intended purpose. Making a gauge swatch isn't required to make a pattern, but my motto is better to play it safe now than waste time making something you can't use.

The first step to checking your gauge is making a gauge swatch using the hook, yarn, and stitch recommended in the pattern. Gauge is typically measured over a 4-inch (10-cm) square. To get the most accurate measurement, make a square that is slightly larger, perhaps a 6-inch (15-cm) square, so the resulting measurement does not include the edge stitches. The pattern should note whether the gauge is taken using a blocked or unblocked swatch.

Measure your gauge by laying the swatch on a flat surface. Using a ruler, count the number of stitches and rows within a 4-inch (10-cm) measurement or the measurement stated in the pattern gauge. There may be partial stitches or rows in this measurement. Be sure to count them too.

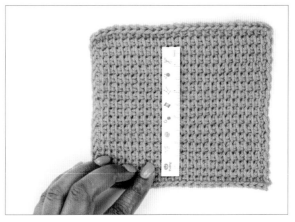

Compare your result to that of the pattern. If you meet the gauge as written, you are good to go and can begin the pattern. If your stitch count or row count is a bit off, it's time to make some adjustments.

ADJUSTMENTS

Meeting a pattern's written gauge on the first try is like finding a golden ticket. It rarely happens to even seasoned crocheters, so don't get discouraged if you have to make adjustments to your tools or project to meet the correct tension. I recommend making a new gauge swatch with each adjustment. Note that changing hook sizes or adjusting row counts may impact the amount of yarn you end up using.

TOO MANY ROWS. If gauge is 12 rows to 4 inches (10 cm) and you get 15 rows in 4 inches (10 cm), your row gauge is too tight. You may need to use more rows within the body of the pattern. Keep your tape measure handy!

TOO FEW ROWS. If gauge is 12 rows to 4 inches (10 cm) and you get 9 rows in 4 inches (10 cm), your row gauge is too loose. You may need to use less rows within the body of the pattern. Keep your tape measure handy!

TOO MANY STITCHES. If gauge is 12 stitches to 4 inches (10 cm) and you get 15 stitches in 4 inches (10 cm), your gauge is too tight. Try going up 0.5–1.0 mm on your next gauge swatch.

TOO FEW STITCHES. If gauge is 12 stitches to 4 inches (10 cm) and you get 9 stitches in 4 inches (10 cm), your gauge is too loose. Try going down 0.5–1.0 mm on your next gauge swatch.

YARN SUBSTITUTIONS

The yarn weight system refers to the thickness of a strand of yarn and places it in a category. But not all yarns are created equal.

Two yarns from different brands might both be a category 4 (worsted weight), but their resulting gauge may differ slightly. This slight difference multiplied over hundreds or thousands of stitches can have unintended results. Be especially vigilant in creating a gauge swatch and making adjustments when you are using a different yarn than what is recommended in the pattern.

RECOMMENDED HOOK SIZES

It's a great idea to experiment with Tunisian crochet when you are just learning. Because of Tunisian crochet's tighter tension compared to traditional crochet, it is generally recommended to use a hook that is 1.0–2.0 mm larger than what is called for on the yarn's ball band when making Tunisian crochet fabric. If you choose to forgo a pattern (or maybe you're making up your own design!), here's a quick guide to recommended hook sizes for an even, medium tension:

YARN CATEGORY	YARN NAMES	TRADITIONAL HOOK SIZE (MM)	TUNISIAN HOOK SIZE (MM)
0 – Lace	Lace, 10-count crochet thread	1.4–1.6	2.5–4
1 – Super Fine	Sock, fingering, baby	2.25–3.5	3–5
2 – Fine	Sport, baby	3.5–4.5	4–6
3 – Light	DK, light worsted	4.5–5.5	5–7
4 – Medium	Worsted, afghan, Aran	5.5–6.5	6–8
5 – Bulky	Chunky, bulky, craft, rug	6.5–9	7–11
6 – Super Bulky	Super bulky, roving	9–15	10–15
7 – Jumbo	Jumbo, roving	15+	15+

Building the Foundation

Lucky you—it's finally time to grab your hooks and get stitching! This section references many of the techniques and actions found in most Tunisian crochet patterns. If this is your first time picking up a hook, give yourself some grace as you are learning. Remember, practice makes progress.

HOLDING THE HOOK

Holding and maneuvering a long Tunisian crochet hook is very different from using a traditional crochet hook. Even if you are an experienced crocheter, you may have to adjust your hold to crochet comfortably and achieve even tension.

Begin by holding the hook in your dominant hand. Your thumb and forefinger will twist and guide the hook through the stitches, while your remaining fingers will maintain balance. Very few Tunisian crochet hooks have thumb rests, so you will need to adjust your hold to a comfortable position without one.

When it comes to holding your yarn, there is no right or wrong way to do it. Hold the yarn in whatever way is most comfortable for you while still allowing you to easily feed yarn to your growing project. This usually means threading the yarn over and around a few of your fingers. I find it easiest to wrap the yarn around the forefinger of my opposite hand twice to maintain even tension.

MAKING A SLIPKNOT

Ninety-nine percent of the time you will begin your project with a slipknot, which is how we connect the yarn to the hook.

(1)   Hold the tail of the yarn in your palm and secure it there with your ring and pinky fingers.

(2)   Wrap the yarn around your forefinger twice, first close to your second knuckle, and then again but closer to your first knuckle. Hold the working yarn with your thumb and middle finger.

(3)   Bring the first loop over the second loop and hold it there.

(4)   Bring the second loop over the first loop and off your fingertip. The first loop remains on your forefinger.

(5)   Pull the tail and working yarn firmly apart to tighten the knot under your forefinger.

(6)   Drop the loop from your forefinger and place it on your hook. Pull firmly on the tail of the slipknot to bring it snug against the hook.

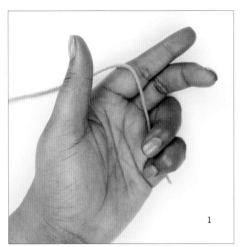

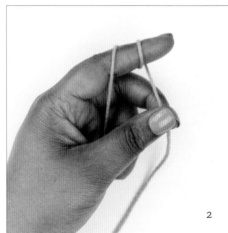

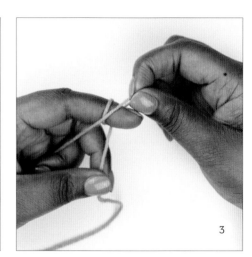

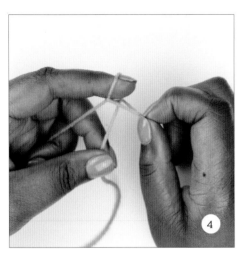

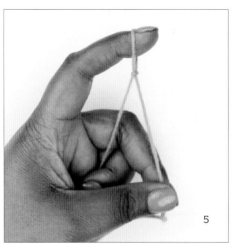

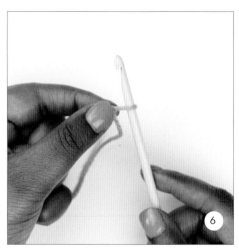

FOUNDATION ROW

The foundation row encompasses three elements: the starting chain, a forward pass, and a return pass. This collection of steps is special because they are the "foundation" upon which the rest of the project is built. Unless you are working in the round, the front (or right side) of the work is always facing you and you do not need to turn your work.

Chain (abbreviated *ch*)—A pattern will tell you how many chains to start with. This is typically the width of your project. If this is a practice piece, start with twelve chains. Count the number of chains by identifying the small v's that are along the chain. One v counts as one chain. Do not count the loop on the hook as a chain.

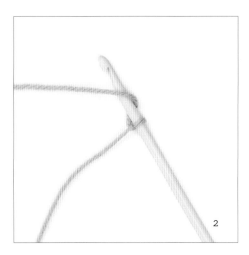

(1) Make a slipknot and place it on your hook.

(2) Make a yarn over by bringing the working yarn over the front of the hook.

(3) Adjust the hook to pull the yarn over through the loop that is on the hook.

(4) Repeat steps 2 and 3 for the number of chains to start the pattern.

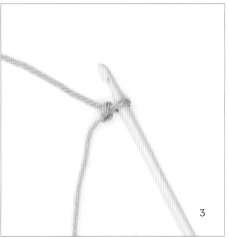

NOTE: In this book, we focus on working Tunisian crochet flat and in the round. The front (or right side) of the work is always facing you, and you do not need to flip over the work between rows.

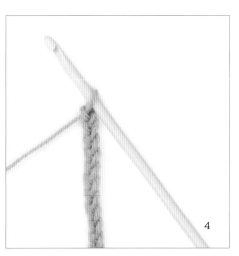

Forward Pass (abbreviated *FwdP*)—The Forward Pass involves gathering loops onto the hook. This is done by pulling up a loop in the starting chain then leaving that loop on the hook as you advance along the row. The hook will move from right to left across the row.

(1) Rotate the starting chain so you are looking at the back bumps along the chain.

(2) Insert your hook into the back bump of the 2nd chain from the hook.

(3) Yarn over with the working yarn.

(4) Pull the yarn through the back bump of the chain. You should now have 2 loops on your hook. Each of these loops counts as a stitch.

(5) Find the next bump along the chain. Insert your hook into that bump, yarn over, and pull up a loop.

(6) Continue pulling up loops until you've done so for each chain. You should have 12 loops on your hook. This completes the forward pass.

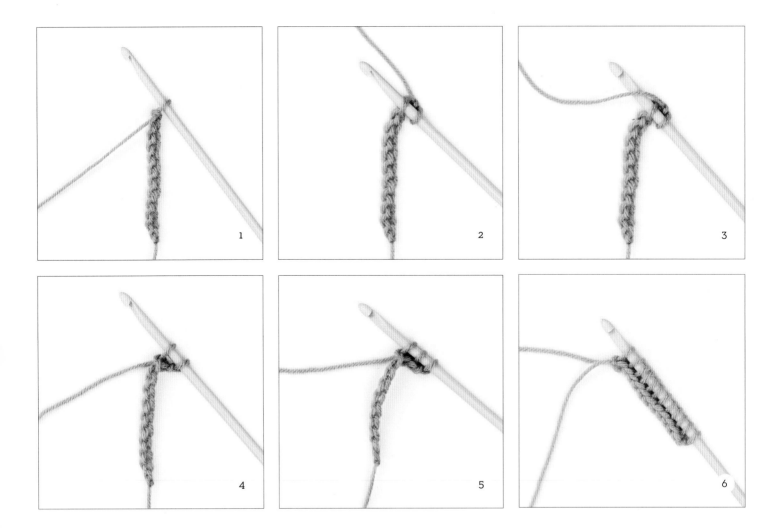

Return Pass (abbreviated *RetP*)—The return pass involves grouping stitches together to work loops off your hook. We will accomplish this by working stitches together after our yarn overs. The hook will progress from left to right across the row.

(1) Yarn over the hook and pull through one loop. This is a chain-1 and helps establish the correct height of your stitches.

(2) Yarn over and pull through the next 2 loops on the hook.

(3) Repeat step 2 until there is only one loop left on the hook. This completes the return pass.

NOTE: This set of instructions is often called the standard return pass, as this same series of steps is used as the return pass for the majority of Tunisian crochet stitches.

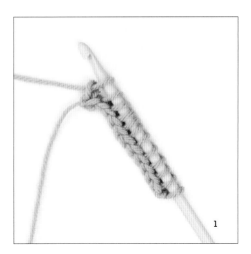

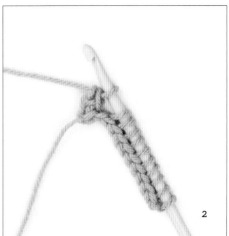

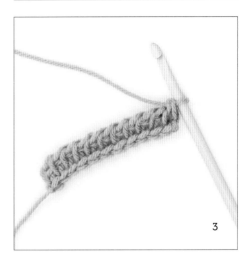

Bind Off

After you are done stitching your project, binding off will give you a neat edge by managing the remaining live loops. There are many ways to bind off, but the most common way is a slip stitch bind off worked under the front vertical bar of the stitches.

(1) Insert your hook under the front vertical bar of the next stitch.

(2) Yarn over the hook.

(3) Pull through both loops on the hook.

(4) Repeat these steps across the row for each stitch.

NOTE: Insert your hook under both loops of the last stitch before completing the slip stitch for a consistent edge.

A bind off worked in the front vertical bars will produce an edge that mimics Tunisian simple stitch. To achieve an edge that looks more like your pattern's stitch, pull up a loop as for the stitch type you were working before completing the slip stitch.

For example, if your pattern is worked in Tunisian knit stitch, complete the bind off as follows: Insert the hook between the two vertical bars, yarn over, pull up a loop, then pull through the loop on the hook.

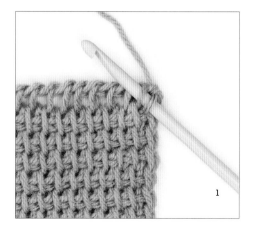

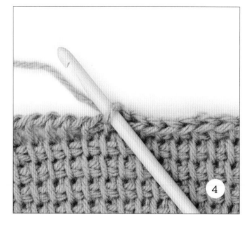

Identifying Loops

When making Tunisian crochet stitches, the instructions might say, "pull up a loop in the front vertical bar" or "insert the hook between the front and back bar." Being able to identify the different loops of a stitch helps to create different stitch patterns, incorporates shaping into a piece, and makes finishing much easier. A Tunisian crochet stitch consists of five loops, which are most easily identified in a Tunisian simple stitch:

Front vertical bar (1)—Often referred to as the "vertical bar," this loop sits to the far left of the stitch at the front of the work.

Back vertical bar (2)—This loop sits just to the right of the front vertical bar, toward the back of the work.

Top bar (3)—The top bar is a horizontal loop that lies perpendicular to the vertical bars.

Bottom bar (4)—The bottom bar is a horizontal loop as well, and it lies just below the top bar.

Back bar (5)—To find the back bar, tilt the top of the working row toward you. You'll find the back bar nestled just behind where the front vertical bar and top bar meet.

STITCHES

Overview

So far, we've mastered reading patterns, controlling our hooks, and building a foundation. We'll employ all of these skills to combine a series of stitches into Tunisian crochet fabric. Each of these patterns builds off the initial foundation row.

Stitches are differentiated by where the hook is inserted, where the working yarn is placed, and sometimes by slight changes in the return pass. By adjusting these small things, we can make hundreds of Tunisian crochet stitch variations.

This section is not an exhaustive list of stitches. Rather, it is a primer to get you comfortable with the movement of making stitches and to prepare you for the designs to come.

All of these stitches begin with a foundation row. They are then worked in rows with a set of forward pass and return pass instructions. Completing one forward pass followed by one return pass is considered one row in a pattern.

If you get lost along the way while practicing these stitch patterns, count the loops on the hook after completing the last stitch of the forward pass. The number of loops on your hook should match the number of stitches in your foundation. If the numbers do not match, drop your hook from the loops, insert your hook into the first loop of the row, pull the working yarn to undo the remaining loops, and start the forward pass again.

NOTE: The first loop on your hook at the beginning of the forward pass counts as the first stitch. As such, skip the first vertical bar at the right edge of your work and always begin the forward pass in the second stitch of the row. When counting your stitches, count the first loop on your hook as number one.

LAST TUNISIAN STITCH (Lts)

The final stitch on the forward pass in Tunisian crochet is worked the same way for most stitch patterns. Working this stitch properly will ensure clean edges along the left-hand side of your work.

When it comes to written patterns, designers often take liberty with how this set of instructions is written, if instructions are given at all. Sometimes you may see "work last stitch" or "work end stitch." I've taken to calling this set of instructions "Last Tunisian stitch," which I abbreviate as *Lts*.

(1) When you reach the last stitch of the row, hold the edge of the work between your thumb and middle finger and rotate the edge toward you.

(2) Insert the hook under BOTH loops of the edge stitch, pushing the hook toward the back of the work.

(3) Yarn over and pull up a loop.

LAST TUNISIAN STITCH (Lts)

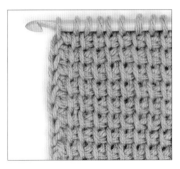

TUNISIAN SIMPLE STITCH (Tss)

Worked over any number of stitches

The Tunisian simple stitch is like the knit stitch of knitting or the single crochet of crocheting. This basic stitch, often called afghan stitch, creates a smooth, gridded fabric. Tunisian simple stitch has a tendency to curl, due to stitches consistently being pulled to the front of the work.

FORWARD: Insert your hook from right to left under the front vertical bar of the 2nd stitch, yarn over, and pull up a loop. Keep the loop on the hook. Continue in this way, pulling up a loop in the front vertical bar of the next stitch to gather loops across the row to the last stitch. Work the Lts.

RETURN: Work the standard return pass (see page 23).

TUNISIAN SIMPLE STITCH (Tss)

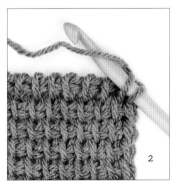

TUNISIAN FULL STITCH (Tfs)

Worked over any number of stitches

The Tunisian full stitch involves pulling up loops between stitches. It is worked in two parts to keep the edges straight. As a stitch pattern, it creates a smooth fabric of vertical bars. As an individual stitch, it can be used as an increase method—more on that in the Shaping section (see page 54).

FORWARD, ROW 1: Insert your hook in the space between the 1st and 2nd stitch, pushing the hook toward the back of the work. Yarn over and pull up a loop. Keep the loop on the hook. Insert the hook in the next space between stitches, yarn over, and pull up a loop. Keep the loop on the hook. Continue in this way, collecting loops, until you get to the space before the last stitch. Skip this space. Work the Lts.

RETURN: Work the standard return pass.

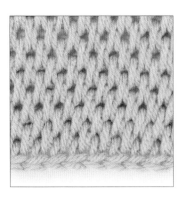

FORWARD, ROW 2: Skip the space between the 1st stitch and the 2nd stitch. Insert hook into the space between the 2nd and 3rd stitch, pushing the hook toward the back of the work. Yarn over and pull up a loop. Keep the loop on the hook. Continue in this way, collecting loops in the spaces between stitches, being sure to pull up a loop in the space before the last stitch. Work the Lts.

RETURN: Work the standard return pass.

Repeat these two rows to form the stitch pattern.

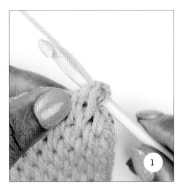

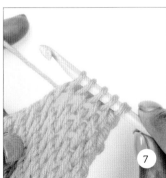

TUNISIAN KNIT STITCH (Tks)

Worked over any number of stitches

Though called the knit stitch, this stitch is actually Tunisian crochet worked in a way that looks deceptively like the knit Stockinette stitch pattern. Due to its structure, this stitch is very dense and creates an even tighter tension than other Tunisian crochet stitches. As such, you may want to increase your hook size even more than usual. And be prepared for some major curling.

FORWARD: Insert your hook between the front and back vertical bars of the stitch, pushing the hook toward the back of the work. Yarn over and pull up a loop. Keep the loop on the hook. Continue in this way, gathering loops across the row to the last stitch. Work the Lts.

RETURN: Work the standard return pass.

TUNISIAN KNIT STITCH (Tks)

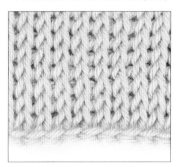

TUNISIAN PURL STITCH (Tps)

Worked over any number of stitches

The Tunisian purl stitch is a beauty on its own, but it is often paired with other stitches to create an interesting textured fabric. I also love using the Tunisian purl stitch as a border on shawls and blankets.

FORWARD: Bring the yarn forward to the front of the work. Insert the hook into the front vertical bar of the next stitch as for Tunisian simple stitch. Bring the working yarn across the vertical bar and to the back of the work. Yarn over and pull up a loop. Keep the loop on the hook. Continue in this way, gathering loops across the row to the last stitch. Work the Lts.

RETURN: Work the standard return pass.

SEED STITCH

Worked over any even number of stitches

The Tunisian crochet seed stitch is a take on the knitted seed stitch, which alternates knit and purl stitches. But the Tunisian seed stitch has a texture all its own. The resulting fabric is flexible with a closed texture.

Special Stitches

- Tunisian knit stitch
- Tunisian purl stitch

FORWARD, ROW 1: Beginning in the 2nd stitch of the row, (tks 1, tps 1) across the row to the last stitch. Work the Lts.

RETURN: Work the standard return pass.

FORWARD, ROW 2: Beginning in the 2nd stitch of the row, (tps 1, tks 1) across the row to the last stitch. Work the Lts.

RETURN: Work the standard return pass.

Repeat these 2 rows to form the stitch pattern.

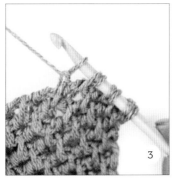

EXTENDED TUNISIAN SIMPLE STITCH (Etss)

Worked over any number of stitches

Extended stitches are like a hidden treasure in Tunisian crochet. Aside from looking great, the extended Tunisian simple stitch has the added benefits of reducing the curl, adding drape and stretch to fabric, and adding height to your rows. To account for the taller stitches, an extra chain-1 is added to the beginning and end of each row.

FORWARD, ROW 1: Ch 1. Tss the 2nd stitch of the row, ch 1. (Tss 1, ch 1) across, gathering loops along the row to the last stitch. Work the Lts in the ch-1 made after the Lts in the previous row, ch 1. **RETURN:** Ch 1 (this is in addition to the ch-1 that begins the standard return pass). Work the standard return pass.

FORWARD, REMAINING ROWS: Ch 1. Tss the 2nd stitch of the row, ch 1. (Tss 1, ch 1) across, gathering loops along the row to the last stitch. To work the last stitch, pull up a loop under 2 loops of the chain after the Lts of the previous row, ch 1. **RETURN:** Ch 1 (this is in addition to the ch-1 that begins the standard return pass). Work the standard return pass.

EXTENDED TUNISIAN SIMPLE STITCH (Etss)

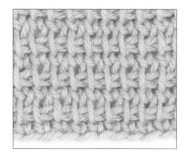

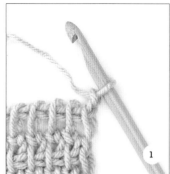

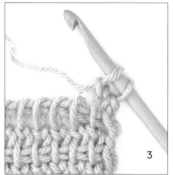

ARROWHEAD STITCH

Worked over any even number of stitches

The arrowhead is a beautiful stitch with a lightly open texture made from yarn over spaces. A combination of stitches and techniques sets this stitch apart from others, making it versatile over a countless number of projects.

Special Stitches

- Tunisian simple stitch
- Tunisian knit stitch
- Tunisian simple stitch 2 together (*tss2tog*): Insert the hook from right to left under the front vertical bars of the next 2 stitches, yarn over, pull up a loop in both stitches together, keep the loop on the hook.

ARROWHEAD STITCH

FORWARD, ROW 1: Tss2tog over the 2nd and 3rd stitch, yo, (tss2tog, yo) across row to last st, Lts.

RETURN: Work the standard return pass.

FORWARD, ROW 2: Tss the 2nd stitch, then insert the hook into the next yarn over space as for tks and pull up a loop. (Tss the next st, tks the yo) across row to last st, Lts.

RETURN: Work the standard return pass.

Repeat these 2 rows to form the stitch pattern.

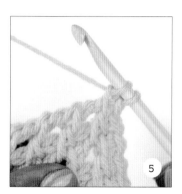

LATTICE STITCH

Worked over any odd number of stitches

Achieve the decorative diagonal line of the lattice stitch by using strategically placed decreases. You will maintain your stitch count by accommodating for each decrease with an additional Tunisian simple stitch.

Special Stitches

- Tunisian simple stitch
- Tunisian simple stitch 2 together (**tss2tog**): Insert the hook from right to left under the front vertical bars of the next 2 stitches, yarn over, pull up a loop in both stitches together, keep the loop on the hook.

FORWARD, ROW 1: Tss2tog over the 2nd and 3rd stitch, tss the first stitch of the tss2tog, (tss2tog, tss the first stitch of the tss2tog) across the row until there are 2 stitches left. Tss the next stitch. Work the Lts.

RETURN: Work the standard return pass.

FORWARD, ROW 2: Tss the 2nd stitch, (tss2tog over the next 2 stitches, tss the first stitch of the tss2tog) across row to last stitch. Work the Lts.

RETURN: Work the standard return pass.

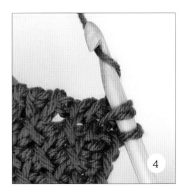

CHEVRON STITCH

Worked over a multiple of 18 stitches

Chevrons are a classic stitch pattern in both knitting and traditional crochet, and you can achieve the same pattern in Tunisian crochet. The basic chevron stitch uses Tunisian simple stitch decreases and yarn overs to achieve the pattern's easily recognizable peaks and valleys.

Special Stitches

- Tunisian simple stitch
- Tss2tog: Tunisian simple stitch 2 together (*tss2tog*): Insert the hook from right to left under the front vertical bars of the next 2 stitches, yarn over, pull up a loop in both stitches together, keep the loop on the hook.

FORWARD: Yo, skip the first vertical bar, *tss 6, tss2tog twice, tss 6, yo**, tss 2, yo; repeat from * across the row to the last st, ending the last repeat at **. Work the Lts.

RETURN: Work the standard return pass.

HONEYCOMB STITCH

Worked over any even number of stitches

The honeycomb stitch pattern is a combination of the Tunisian simple stitch and the Tunisian purl stitch, both of which are explained earlier in this section. The resulting fabric looks to have small depressions surrounded by a honeycomb pattern, hence the name. The honeycomb stitch creates a thinner fabric than the Tunisian simple stitch, and it has the added benefit of not curling at all.

Special Stitches

- Tunisian simple stitch
- Tunisian purl stitch

FORWARD, ROW 1: Beginning with the 2nd stitch of the row, (tss 1, tps 1) across the row to the last stitch. Work the Lts.
RETURN: Work the standard return pass.

FORWARD, ROW 2: Beginning in the 2nd stitch of the row, (tps 1, tss 1) across the row to the last stitch. Work the Lts.
RETURN: Work the standard return pass.
Repeat these 2 rows to form the stitch pattern.

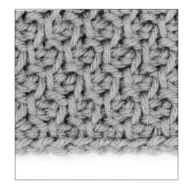

Traditional Crochet Stitches and Techniques

Elements of traditional crochet can be helpful throughout a Tunisian crochet pattern. In *The Tunisian Crochet Handbook*, traditional crochet is used to adjust direction, set up rows, and aid in finishing. These techniques aren't routinely used when practicing Tunisian crochet, but this basic knowledge will help you fly through tricky parts of a pattern.

FRONT AND BACK LOOPS

The tops of crochet stitches are comprised of two loops—a front loop and a back loop. Crochet stitches are worked under both loops unless otherwise stated.

Working in the front loop only is abbreviated *fl* for *FLO* and references the loop that is closest to you, while working in the back loop only is abbreviated *bl* or *BLO* and references the loop that is farthest from you.

For example, "sc BLO in the next 6 sts" means to single crochet in the back loop only for each of the next six stitches.

SLIP STITCH (Sl st)

(1) Insert the hook into the next stitch.

(2) Yarn over.

(3) Pull the loop through the stitch and the loop that is on the hook.

SINGLE CROCHET (Sc)

(1) Insert the hook into the next stitch.

(2) Yarn over.

(3) Pull up a loop (2 loops on the hook).

(4) Yarn over.

(5) Pull through both loops on the hook.

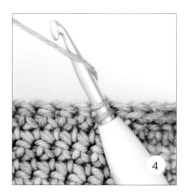

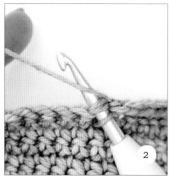

REVERSE SINGLE CROCHET (Reverse sc)

The reverse single crochet is worked just like a normal single crochet but in reverse, from left to right for right-handed crocheters and from right to left for left-handed crocheters.

(1) Insert the hook from front to back into the stitch to the right of the hook for right-handed crocheters and to the left of the hook for left-handed crocheters.

(2) Yarn over.

(3) Pull up a loop (2 loops on the hook).

(4) Yarn over.

(5) Pull through both loops on hook.

MAGIC RING (MR)

The magic ring (also called magic loop or magic circle) is an adjustable loop that allows you to make stitches for starting projects worked in the round. Once all stitches are added, the tail end of the loop is pulled tight to prevent a hole in the center of the work. There are several ways to make a magic ring. This is my preferred method, with a technique that nearly mirrors the slipknot directions from the Building the Foundation section (see page 19).

(1) Hold the tail of the yarn in your palm and secure it there with your ring and pinky fingers.

(2) Wrap the yarn around your forefinger twice, first close to your second knuckle, and then again but closer to your first knuckle. Hold the working yarn with your thumb and middle finger.

(3) Bring the first loop over the second and hold it there.

(4) Bring the second loop over the first and off your fingertip.

(5) Pull the tail and working yarn firmly apart to tighten the knot below your finger.

(6) Drop the loop from your finger and place it on your hook. The knot should be resting on top of the hook with the working yarn to the left and the yarn tail to the right.

(7) Yarn over and pull up a loop in the ring. This does not count as a chain. Proceed to the next instructions in the pattern.

1

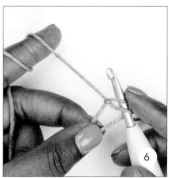

2

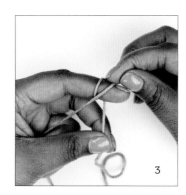

3

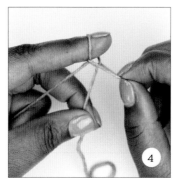

4

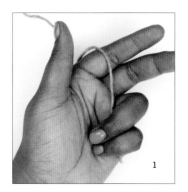

5

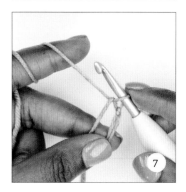

6

7

WORKING INTO THE MAGIC RING

After creating the magic ring, the pattern will give instructions on how many stitches to place in that ring, usually starting with a number of chain stitches. Stitches are worked around the yarn that comprises the loop. For this example, we'll work one chain and six single crochet.

(1) Yarn over and pull up a loop (chain-1 complete).

(2) Insert the hook into the ring.

(3) Yarn over and pull up a loop (2 loops on the hook).

(4) Yarn over.

(5) Pull through both loops on hook (single crochet complete).

(6) Repeat steps 2–5 five more times (6 single crochet in the ring).

(7) Pull the tail of the magic ring firmly to close the hole. The last single crochet made should now be nearly touching the first single crochet of the round.

Proceed to the next instructions in the pattern.

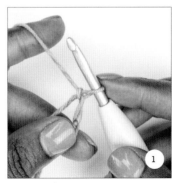

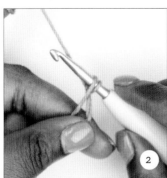

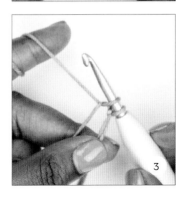

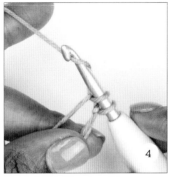

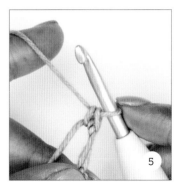

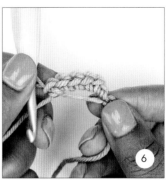

CROCHETING A FLAT SPIRAL

Now that the first round of stitches is in the magic ring, you can build on these stitches by placing increases while working in a spiral. To keep the circle flat, increases are spaced out evenly and become farther apart as the circle grows. It is helpful to use a locking stitch marker to identify the end of the round so you do not lose count. For this example, we'll work two single crochet into each stitch around.

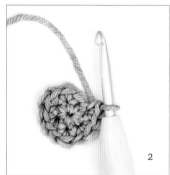

(1) Without turning your work, place 2 single crochet in the next stitch to the left, or right for left-handed crocheters.

(2) Continue placing 2 single crochet in each of the 6 single crochet stitches around.

Once complete, there should be 12 single crochet stitches in the round. If you are using a stitch marker, this is a good time to move it up to mark the new round.

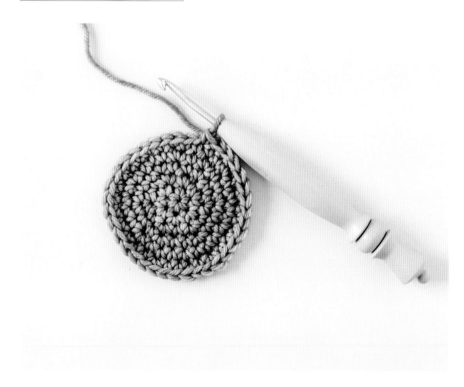

CROCHETING JOINED ROUNDS

The flat spiral mentioned in the previous instructions can be used to create the base of a project. In this case, joined rounds are built upon the flat spiral to make the sides. The end of a round is joined to the beginning of a round using a slip stitch. The round starts with a series of chains, then transitions into crochet stitches. For this example, we will work one chain to start the round, then single crochet in each stitch around.

(1) Yarn over and pull up a loop (chain-1 complete).

(2) Single crochet in the first stitch and in each stitch of the round.

(3) At the end of the round, once all single crochet stitches are complete, insert your hook under both loops of the first single crochet of the round.

(4) Yarn over and pull through all the loops on the hook to join the round with a slip stitch.

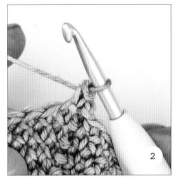

THE APPLIED RIBBING TECHNIQUE

This technique allows you to add single crochet ribbing to any edge of Tunisian crochet fabric. It's a great finishing choice for hats, garments, and even blankets. The ribbing is worked perpendicular to the Tunisian crochet fabric by continually picking up stitches. For this example, we will make an applied ribbing that is 5 stitches long.

(1) Place a slipknot on your hook.

(2) Insert the hook into the first stitch on the right-hand side of your work.

(3) Yarn over and pull up a loop through both the stitch and the loop on your hook (slip stitch complete).

(4) Ch 6.

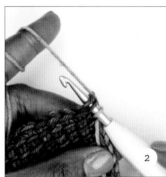

(5) Single crochet in the 2nd chain from the hook and in each of the remaining chains. You will have 5 single crochet stitches.

(6) Slip stitch into the same stitch as the join.

(7) Slip stitch into the next stitch along the edge.

(8) Turn your work so you are now looking at the back of the stitches you just made.

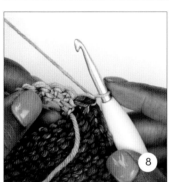

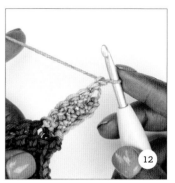

(9) Skip both slip stitches and single crochet in the back loop of the next single crochet.

(10) Sc in BLO in each single crochet along the row.

(11) Turn your work so you are looking at the back of the stitches you just made.

(12) Ch 1.

(13) Sc in BLO in each single crochet along the row.

(14) Slip stitch in each of the next 2 stitches along the edge. Repeat steps 9–14 along the row edge. End with step 10 or step 14 as needed to complete the ribbing.

SKILLS

Adding Color

Adding even one more color to your Tunisian crochet projects has the ability to change the tone of your finished piece. Color can create pictures, portray a mood, draw the eye, and personalize even the simplest patterns. This section outlines several different ways to add color when working with Tunisian crochet.

While you can add color to practically any stitch, most of these techniques work best on smooth, basic stitches like Tunisian simple stitch, Tunisian knit stitch, and Tunisian full stitch. Experiment with adding color while working with your stitch swatches.

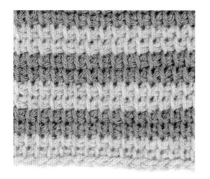

STRIPES

Create stripes in your work by completing the forward and return pass in the same color, then changing to an accent color at the end of the return pass. If you are repeating colors for stripes in subsequent rows, carry the yarn up the side of the work for a maximum of four rows to maintain the proper gauge.

Complete the return pass until there are two loops left on the hook. Drop the current color, yarn over with the new color, and pull through both loops on the hook. There is now one loop on the hook, which counts as the first stitch of the new row.

TWO-TONE STRIPES

One of my favorite unique features of Tunisian crochet is the two-tone stripe. Tunisian crochet rows are made up of two parts—the forward and return passes. By working these passes in different colors, a pleasing mix of color is achieved.

Complete the forward pass in your chosen color, working through the Last Tunisian stitch. Drop the current color, yarn over with the accent color, and pull up a loop. This counts at the chain-1 of the return pass. Complete the return pass with the accent color. To continue the two-tone stripes, complete the next forward pass with the accent color, then change back to the main color to begin the return pass.

CHANGING COLOR MID-ROW

This type of color change is seen most often with intarsia and stranded colorwork. Changing color this way creates a crisp line. Stitch patterns like Tunisian simple stitch and Tunisian knit stitch are often used for this type of color change, allowing the maker to add text and pictures to Tunisian crochet fabric.

When you reach the stitch where you are meant to change color on the forward pass, drop the main color, insert the hook into the next stitch, yarn over with the new color, and pull up the loop. Complete the remainder of the row or the appropriate number of stitches with the accent color. Complete the return pass until there is only one loop left of the accent color. Yarn over and pull up through the next two loops with the main color and complete the return pass as normal.

FRONT   BACK

STRANDED COLORWORK

This style of managing color works best when two or more colors are used multiple times in a single row. You will typically find stranded colorwork represented in a chart that creates a picture by working from the bottom of the chart to the top, with rows read from right to left.

Stranded colorwork involves carrying the unused color behind the active row, creating "floats" on the back of the work. As colors change from the main color to the accent within the same row, the two strands of yarn are carried along the row and switched out as needed. Floats should rest gently on the back of your work and should not be too long. Mismanaging floats could cause snags or major problems with tension.

If only two colors are used in this way, the resulting fabric is akin to Fair Isle in knitting. It can be a little fiddly, but it is possible to manage several colors at a time during stranded colorwork.

Stranded colorwork is accomplished using the same premise as changing color mid-row. When you reach the stitch to change color on the forward pass, drop the main color, insert the hook into the stitch, and pull up the loop with the accent color. When it is time to change color again during the forward pass of the same row, drop the accent color and yarn over with the main color, being sure not to pull the yarn too tightly.

Work the return pass as normal, changing color when there is only one loop of the active color left on the hook.

Depending on the pattern, you may have long stretches of stitches worked in only one color. To address the unused yarn in these sections, try "locking the float" every five to six stitches on both the forward pass and the return pass. To lock the float, wrap the yarn that is not in use around the working yarn. This will create a short float with the yarn that is not in use and will make it easier to maintain your tension once it is time to crochet with that color again.

FRONT   BACK

INTARSIA

In the case where floats would be inconvenient or multiple colors are getting too complicated to handle, try the intarsia technique. This style of colorwork is best for larger blocks of a single color while still allowing you to change color in the middle of a row. Like stranded colorwork, intarsia color changes are typically shown in chart form and read from bottom to top, with rows read from right to left.

Instead of carrying yarn throughout a row, only one color is used at a time. Unused colors are still attached to the project, but they remain where they are left until they are needed again.

For projects using multiple colors, keep each ball of yarn accessible or wind yarn into individual bobbins for each color. If the same color is present multiple times in a row, create a separate bobbin for each instance of that color.

As with changing color mid-row, drop the main color on the forward pass when it is time for a color change. Insert the hook into the next stitch, yarn over with the new color, and pull up a loop. Continue in the pattern for the number of stitches indicated with the accent color. When you reach another color change, drop the current color and work the next stitch with the new color, leaving the unused color attached to the project.

Complete the return pass as normal, changing color when there is only one loop of the current color on the hook. Yarn over with the strand of the new color that is attached to the project, bringing the new color under the strand of the previous color. Locking the strands in place this way on the return pass prevents any holes in your work.

Shaping

There are myriad ways to create shape in Tunisian crochet fabric. Easily increase or decrease in rows. Add multiple stitches to the beginning or end of rows. Gently change direction using short rows. Every technique has its perks, and the appropriate time to use a certain skill depends on the effect you are trying to achieve.

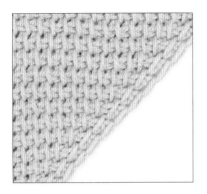

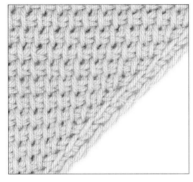

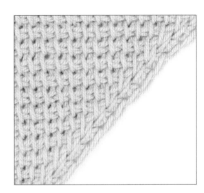

INCREASING

Back Bar Increase—Insert the hook into the bump above and slightly behind the front vertical bar of the next stitch. This loop can be a little tough to grab—it may help to use the nail of your index finger to assist getting the loop onto the hook. Yarn over and pull up a loop to complete the increase. From here, continue in pattern. The vertical bar below the bump is considered the next stitch.

Yarn Over Increase—Where indicated, yarn over the hook, then move on to the next stitch. The act of the yarn over creates an additional loop on the hook, thus increasing your overall stitch count.

Full Stitch Increase—Insert the hook into the space between the stitch just worked and the next stitch, pushing the hook toward the back of the work. Yarn over and pull up a loop, thus completing the increase.

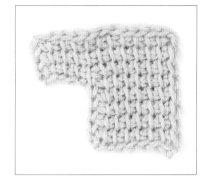

Adding Stitches to the Right-Hand Side—Complete the return pass until there is only one loop left on the hook. Chain the number of stitches you would like to add to the beginning of the row. Pull up a loop in the back bump of the second chain from the hook and in each chain created. When you reach the end of the chain, continue working in the pattern stitch along the original stitches and complete the return pass as normal.

Adding Stitches to the Left-Hand Side—Use a separate length of yarn to create a chain equal to the number of stitches you want to add. Fasten off and set the chain aside. Work on the Tunisian crochet piece until you reach the end of the forward pass and are ready to add stitches. Insert the hook into the back bump of the first stitch on the chain you created. Continue pulling up loops in the back bump of the chain until all chains are worked. Complete the return pass as normal.

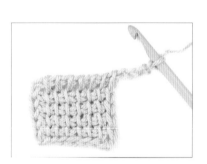

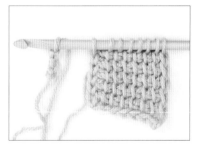

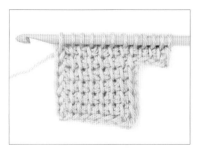

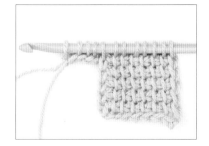

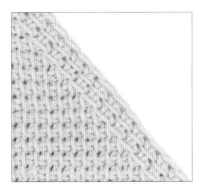

DECREASING

Two Together Decrease—Insert the hook into the next stitch as for Tunisian simple stitch, then insert the hook into the following stitch as for the pattern stitch (e.g., insert under the next vertical bar for tss, then insert between the two vertical bars for tks and so on). Yarn over and pull up a loop through both stitches to complete the decrease.

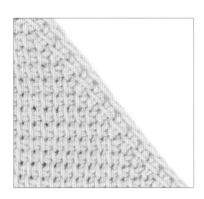

Skip One—Work in pattern during the forward pass to the stitch where the decrease is meant to be made. Skip over that stitch, leaving it unworked, and continue in pattern starting with the next stitch.

Removing Stitches on the Right-Hand Side—At the beginning of the forward pass, slip stitch in the next vertical bar, then in each vertical bar across the row for the number of stitches you need to remove from the work.

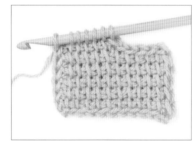

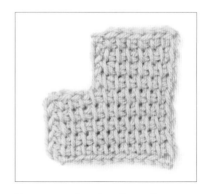

Removing Stitches from the Left-Hand Side—Work along the row during the forward pass up to the stitch where stitches are meant to be removed. Slip stitch in the vertical bars of stitches across for the number of stitches indicated, being sure to insert into the last stitch as for Lts. Once all slip stitches are complete, cut the yarn leaving a tail long enough to weave in. Adjust the hook to continue crocheting in the live stitches. Yarn over and pull up a loop. Complete the return pass as normal.

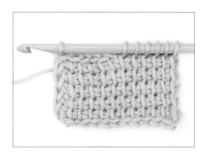

SHORT ROWS

A full row in Tunisian crochet consists of a forward pass and a return pass, both with the same number of stitches. Therefore, a short row is a row worked over a partial number of the stitches from the previous row, leaving the remaining stitches unworked. For example, if a row had fifteen stitches, a short row would be working a forward and return pass over just ten of those fifteen stitches.

Short rows are a great way to add subtle shaping to a Tunisian crochet project. Use short rows to turn a heel on a sock, add darts near the bustline of a garment, or add crescent accents to wraps.

The short row itself is simple—just work a partial number of stitches during the forward pass, followed by the standard return pass. The trick comes in the row following a short row. Working the last stitch of the short row properly will prevent gaps in the work.

Work the forward pass in the pattern stitch for the partial number of stitches instructed in the pattern. Complete the standard return pass, being sure to begin with a chain-1.

For the following row, work in the pattern stitch over the short row stitches to the last stitch. Insert the hook under both loops of the last stitch.

Continue picking up loops along the full length of the row until all stitches are worked. Complete the Lts and the standard return pass.

Working in the Round

When it comes to items like gloves, socks, and even sweaters, working Tunisian crochet in the round makes more sense than working the project in flat rows. Working in the round, specifically in a spiral, creates a seamless fabric that is more appealing than seaming the ends of flat rows.

A double-ended hook is needed to work Tunisian crochet in the round. A rigid hook works fine, but interchangeable hooks attached to a flexible cord will allow you to pick up more stitches on your forward passes and limit the need to flip your work every few stitches.

You will also need two separate balls of yarn for working in the round. One ball will be used for the forward pass while the other is used for the return pass. These two balls can be the same color or two different colors. Using the same color will give you a solid-color fabric. Using two different colors will give you an interesting-looking two-tone fabric.

FOUNDATION ROUND— FORWARD PASS

(1) Use yarn A to chain the required number of stitches.

(2) Without twisting the chain, bring the first chain stitch to the hook, insert the hook into the first chain stitch, and complete a slip stitch to create a ring. The loop on the hook counts as the first stitch—mark it with a stitch marker to keep track of your rounds.

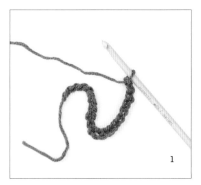

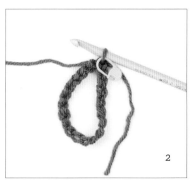

(3) Pull up a loop in the back bump of the next chain stitch and keep the loop on the hook. Repeat for as many chain stitches as you can before the loop becomes taut.

FOUNDATION ROUND— RETURN PASS

(4) Rotate the hook so you are looking at the wrong side of the work. Shift the loops to the opposite end of the hook.

(5) With yarn B, yarn over the hook and pull up a loop.

(6) (Yarn over and pull through two loops) until there is one loop of yarn A and one loop of yarn B on the hook.

(7) Rotate the hook so you are looking at the right side of the work. Shift the loops to the opposite side of the hook to resume the forward pass.

(8) Repeat steps 3–7 as needed until all chains of the foundation are worked.

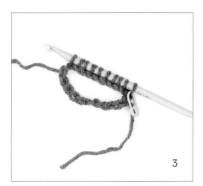

3

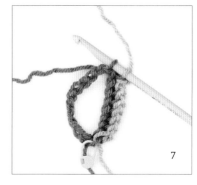

7

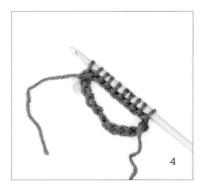

4

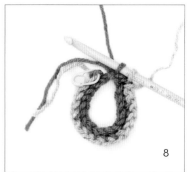

8

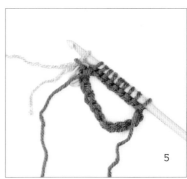

5

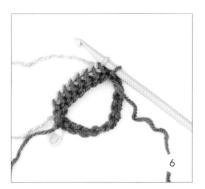

6

SUBSEQUENT ROUNDS—FORWARD PASS

(1) From this point, you can work in the pattern stitch. Assuming the pattern is Tunisian simple stitch, resume the forward pass by inserting the hook into the vertical bar of the first stitch and pulling up a loop. If using a stitch marker, move it up now.

(2) Continue working the forward pass by pulling up loops in the front vertical bars of stitches until the work becomes taut on the hook.

SUBSEQUENT ROUNDS—RETURN PASS

(1) Rotate the hook so you are looking at the wrong side of the work. Shift the loops to the opposite end of the hook.

(2) (Yarn over and pull through two loops) until there is one loop of yarn A and one loop of yarn B on the hook.

(3) Rotate the hook so you are looking at the right side of the work. Shift the loops to the opposite side of the hook to resume the forward pass.

Repeat steps on this page to the desired length, replacing the stitch marker on the first stitch of the round as you go.

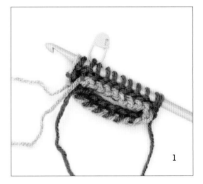

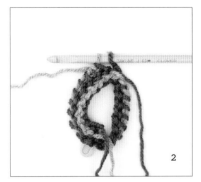

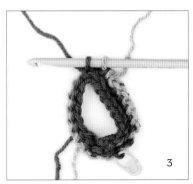

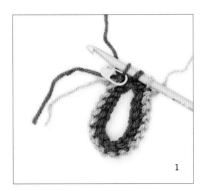

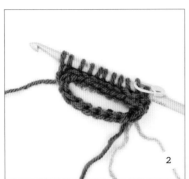

BINDING OFF IN THE ROUND

(1) With the right side of the work facing you, you should have one loop of yarn A and one loop of yarn B on the hook after completing the return pass.

(2) Slip yarn A through yarn B. There is now only one loop of yarn A on the hook. Fasten off yarn B.

(3) Slip stitch loosely in each stitch around to complete the slip stitch bind off. At the end of the round, cut yarn A, leaving enough length to weave in the ends.

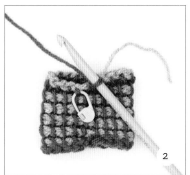

Finishing

Most makers have a love-hate relationship with finishing. And for good reason. While you're technically done stitching, there are still several steps needed to make your project perfect for photographing, gifting, or selling.

FASTENING OFF

One instruction you will see at the end of Tunisian crochet projects is to "fasten off," which usually comes after the bind off. This essentially means to tie off the yarn after the final stitch and separate the project from the yarn ball.

When you are ready to fasten off, cut the yarn from the ball, leaving a tail about 6 inches (15 cm) long. From here, lift the loop up high until the tail pops out of the work. This is the tail we will now weave into the work.

WEAVING IN ENDS

To weave in your ends, thread the end of the tail through a tapestry needle. Flip your work so you are looking at the wrong side. The wrong side of Tunisian crochet has a series of bumps that are perfect for holding on to yarn tails.

Thread the tapestry needle through several bumps in one direction, then several bumps in the opposite direction. Repeat this until the full length of the tail is woven into the back of the fabric. Trim the remaining tail close to the fabric and discard the leftover yarn.

CALMING THE CURL

The number one question most first-time Tunisian crocheters have is how to deal with the curling that happens within the first few rows of most Tunisian crochet projects. Curling is the product of consistently pulling up loops toward the front of the work. For stitches like Tunisian simple stitch and Tunisian knit stitch, curling can be especially frustrating. But we are in luck—there are several different ways to minimize the curl while working Tunisian crochet.

The first line of defense comes with picking the correct hook. As mentioned in the Gauge section (page 17), choose a hook that is at least 1–2 mm larger than what is recommended on the yarn's ball band. If the resulting fabric still curls, try going up another hook size. At some point, you have to balance calming the curl with changing the gauge of your fabric.

Starting and ending your project with a few rows of an alternate stitch can help with curling. Complete a few rows of the honeycomb stitch pattern, extended Tunisian simple stitch, or even the Tunisian purl stitch before moving on to the pattern stitch. The honeycomb and extended stitches lie flat on their own, while the purl stitch curls in the opposite direction of Tunisian simple and knit stitch. In this same spirit, adding a border to

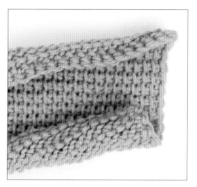

BEFORE BLOCKING

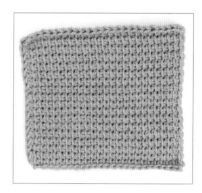

AFTER BLOCKING

the project can help relax the curl, but more on that later.

Considering that curling happens so early in a project, you might be wondering why I'm mentioning it in the finishing section. It's because the absolute best method to calm the curl in Tunisian crochet is blocking. This is my favorite tried-and-true method, but blocking is often overlooked in the crochet community.

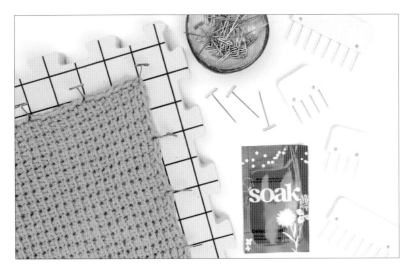

BLOCKING

Even as I write this, I can hear a collective groan from the maker community when it comes to the topic of blocking. Blocking is a process that combines heat, water, and time to help relax stitches, improve the shape, and incorporate drape into finished stitched fabrics. This step requires a bit of patience, but that patience is greatly rewarded when it comes time to actually use the piece you've made.

There are three main types of blocking, each with its own benefits and limitations. Choosing a blocking method will depend on what the finished piece is, how much time you have, and what fiber was used. Experiment with each method, preferably on a gauge swatch, to find the one that works best for you based on the types of projects you like to make.

Spray Block

- Supplies: Blocking boards, rustproof pins, a spray bottle with warm water combined with a touch of wool wash

- How to: Pin the item to the desired finished measurements on the blocking board with rustproof pins. Spray the piece with the warm water and soap solution until it is lightly saturated. Press lightly on the piece to position stitches where you want them to be. Let the piece dry fully before removing from the blocking board.

- Pros: This is typically a quick method and works well for small swatches and motifs like squares. This method is great for those new to blocking, as it is a gentle way to relax the stitches and get a feel for how a particular fiber takes to blocking.

- Cons: This method will not do much for adding to the dimensions of your finished piece. This method is also pretty mild when it comes to blocking, and the finished piece might bounce back to its original dimensions and curl over time.

Steam Block

- Supplies: Blocking boards, rustproof pins, a garment steamer or steam iron

- How to: Pin the item to the desired finished measurements on the blocking board with rustproof pins. Hold the steamer or steam iron 1–2 inches (2.5–5 cm) above the piece and allow the steam to permeate the stitches. Move the steamer over the full piece to ensure all stitches interact with the steam. Allow the piece to fully dry before removing it from the blocking board.

- Pros: Steam blocking works well for just about any fiber and any project. It is slightly more aggressive than spray blocking, so your stitches will stay in place, but not so aggressive that the size and shape of the piece will be inadvertently altered.

- Cons: You have to pay close attention while steam blocking. Allowing the hot surface of the steamer or iron to come in contact with your stitches could ruin your hard work.

You could end up with holes or permanently flattened stitches. Also, keep your fingers away from the metal plate of the iron or steamer. Both get very hot and can burn you.

NOTE ABOUT ACRYLIC YARN: Acrylic yarn can be steam blocked, and it is my preferred method. Acrylic is a man-made fiber and performs much like thin plastic. When steam blocking acrylic yarn, pin the finished piece to the blocking boards with the wrong side facing up. Steam block as normal. Blocking with the wrong side up ensures that you do not flatten the stitches on the right side of the work.

Wet Block

- Supplies: Blocking boards, rustproof pins, a towel, a sink or large basin, wool wash

- How to: Fill the sink with water that is warm to the touch. Add a small amount of wool wash and remove excess bubbles. Fully submerge your finished Tunisian crochet piece in the water and let it set for about twenty minutes. Remove the piece from the water. Squeeze excess water out of the piece, being careful not to wring or twist the fabric. Lay the piece in a single layer on a towel and roll the towel. Press the towel to remove even more water from the piece. Lay the piece on blocking boards.

Lightly stretch and pin it to the finished dimensions. Allow the piece to fully dry before removing it from the blocking board.

- Pros: This method works especially well for animal fibers like wool, cashmere, and alpaca. Immersing fibers allows the water to permeate them, giving them a chance to "bloom" or open up. Fibers blocked this way are bouncy, soft, and smooth while still achieving adjustments in size and drape. Wet blocking has the added benefit of being a washing method for handmade pieces. The use of a light wool wash removes oils and odors from the fabric.

- Cons: There isn't really a downside to wet blocking when you use it for the right projects.

NOTE: Stitches are extremely pliable when they are wet. Take care not to wring, twist, or rub them together, as this can cause felting in animal fibers. Also, Tunisian crochet fabric will try to bounce back into shape while drying. Place several pins along the edges of your work to prevent any unsightly peaks and valleys once the piece dries.

ADDING BORDERS

A crochet border does double duty by adding a decorative element to your finished project while also calming the curl. The first round of a crochet border lays the foundation for the following rows. How you choose to pick up loops and work stitches along the end of your work will impact the overall look of the border. Here are my recommendations for picking up loops around the four edges of Tunisian crochet to prevent small holes in the work:

- Along the top edge: Pull up loops in each slip stitch of the bind off row.

- Along the left edge: Insert the hook between the horizontal bars of the stitch just before the last stitch and pull up a loop.

- Along the bottom edge: Pull up loops in the chain stitches of the foundation row.

- Along the right edge: Insert the hook between the horizontal bars of the first stitch of the row.

Seaming

SLIP STITCH SEAM

Hold the pieces to be joined with their right sides together and the wrong sides facing out. Choose a crochet hook that is the same size as the Tunisian crochet hook used in the project. Insert the hook into the loops of both thicknesses. Inserting the hook into both loops, only the front loops, or only the back loops will give you a different result.

Yarn over with your joining yarn and pull up a loop, being sure to leave a tail to weave in later. The first slip stitch is complete. Insert the hook into the loops of the next stitch for both thicknesses. Yarn over and pull up a loop through the stitches and the loop on the hook. Continue down the edge of the work, placing a slip stitch in both thicknesses of each stitch. Be sure to do this loosely so there is no puckering along your join.

SINGLE CROCHET SEAM

Hold the pieces to be joined with their right sides together and the wrong sides facing out. Choose a crochet hook that is the same size as the Tunisian crochet hook used in the project. Insert the hook into the loops of both thicknesses.

Yarn over with the joining yarn and pull up a loop (slip stitch complete). Chain 1. Single crochet in the same stitch as the join. Single crochet down the edge of the work, being sure to insert the hook into both thicknesses as you work into stitches along the edge.

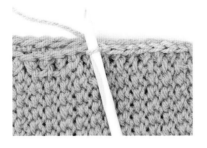

WHIPSTITCH SEAM

Whipstitches can be worked with either the right or the wrong sides of the work facing out. These are sturdy seams that will hold tight throughout handling and washing. Use a coordinating color to make whipstitch seams less obvious.

Hold the pieces to be joined so either the right or wrong sides of both pieces are facing out. Thread a length of yarn through a tapestry needle.

Insert the needle from front to back through both thicknesses of the work, being sure to leave a tail to weave in later. Bring the tapestry needle over the work and position it in the front again. Insert the needle through both thicknesses from front to back of the next stitch. Continue along the edges to join.

MATTRESS SEAM

The mattress seam creates a mostly invisible, sturdy seam. This is ideal for when the seam should be subtle, as with joining pieces of a garment.

Lay the pieces to be seamed with the right sides facing up and the edges facing one another. We'll call the left piece A and the right piece B. Thread a length of yarn through a tapestry needle. Insert the needle from back to front through the bottom stitch of the A edge, then do the same in the corresponding stitch of B. Use the tail to tie a knot at the back of the work to fasten the two pieces together.

Insert the needle under the horizontal bars of the next stitch on the A edge, working from bottom to top, and pull the yarn through. Do the same for the corresponding stitch on B. Continue in this way along the seam.

RUNNING STITCH SEAM

A running stitch seam is a simple way to join two pieces. This can leave a decorative edge, as the v's of the edge stitches face outward.

Lay the pieces to be seamed with their wrong sides facing one another and the right sides facing out. Thread a tapestry needle with a length of yarn.

Insert the needle from front to back through both thicknesses of the work, being sure to leave a tail to weave in later. Insert the needle from back to front through the next stitch. Continue in this way, first weaving from front to back through corresponding stitches, then from back to front through the next stitch.

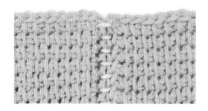

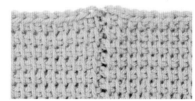

BACKSTITCH SEAM

Seaming using the backstitch results in an extra-strong seam that is still slightly stretchy. If you want the seam to be nearly invisible, work the backstitch with the right sides facing each other and the wrong sides facing out. In this instance, we are using a contrasting color and the right sides facing out to display a decorative edge.

Lay the pieces to be seamed with their wrong sides facing each other and the right sides facing out. Thread a tapestry needle with a length of yarn.

Insert the needle from back to front through both thicknesses one stitch in from the corner, being sure to leave a tail for weaving in later. Insert the needle from front to back through the corner stitches of both pieces. Bring the needle from back to front through the thicknesses of the stitch to the left of the first stitch, then back into the first stitch from front to back. Continue in this way, seaming one stitch to the left when inserting the needle from back to front, then into the stitch to the right when inserting the needle from front to back.

Embellishments

CROSS STITCH

One of the benefits of Tunisian crochet is the smooth fabric it makes. The Tunisian simple stitch provides an ideal canvas for cross stitching pictures and text into fabric. Work cross-stitch designs from a grid, or freestyle your design.

Tunisian simple stitch naturally opens at the places where vertical lines meet. Cross stitches are made in the space toward the inside of this junction to give a consistent and clean look. Achieve this by working the first half of the X along the row, then returning across the row to make the second half of the X. Be mindful that you do not pull any part of the cross stitch too tightly as it will cause the Xs to collapse and distort your finished image.

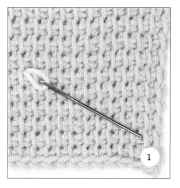

(1) Thread a tapestry needle with a length of your desired contrast-color yarn. Bring the yarn from back to front through the base of the stitch toward the inside of where two vertical bars meet. Leave a tail to weave in later.

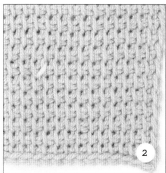

(2) Pass the needle across the stitch and through the space of the outside top of the next bar.

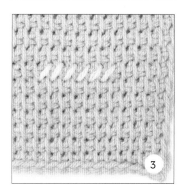

(3) Work diagonally in this way for the number of stitches needed in the pattern. This constitutes the first half of your cross stitches.

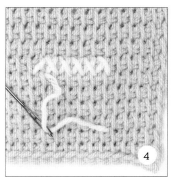

(4) Working in the opposite direction, insert the hook through spaces already worked to complete the X.

POM-POMS

Love them or hate them, pom-poms are here to stay in the crochet community. Yarn pom-poms can adorn the edge of finished projects or be used as a decorative element within the body of a project. There are many methods to make pom-poms, from using cardboard to toilet paper tubes. I prefer to make yarn pom-poms with a dedicated pom-pom maker, as this produces more consistent results over time.

(1) Open one end of the pom-pom maker, holding both arms together.

(2) Wrap the yarn evenly around both arms, working back and forth until the crescent at the base of the arms is filled with yarn. When you are finished wrapping, ensure that the working yarn is at the opposite end of the hinge.

(3) Close the wrapped arms and open the other arms of the pom-pom maker.

(4) Without cutting the yarn, begin wrapping the working yarn around the other arms as done in step 2. When complete, close so that both sets of arms are wrapped with yarn and closed to the pom-pom maker. Cut the working yarn.

(5) Using sharp scissors, work along the outer channel of the pom-pom maker and snip the lengths of yarn.

(6) Cut a long length of yarn from the ball. Fold it in half. Holding the length of yarn double, shimmy it into the channel of the pom-pom maker. Tie the ends of the yarn tightly together several times.

(7) Open both sets of arms and pull the two halves of the pom-pom maker apart to free the pom-pom. At this point, the pom-pom strands are a little uneven. Holding the long tails used to knot the pom-pom, give the pom a shake to fluff it as much as you can.

(8) Hold the base of the knot and use sharp scissors to trim strands until they are even.

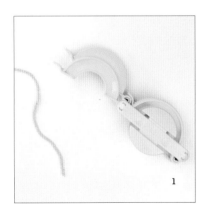

1

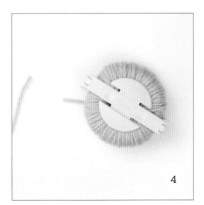

2

3

4

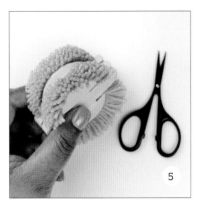

5

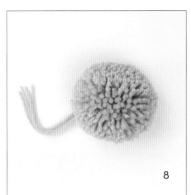

6

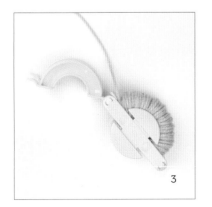

7

8

FRINGE

Fringe can instantly add personality to Tunisian crochet shawls, scarves, and wall hangings. Customize the color, length, and density of your fringe to change the vibe of your project.

(1) Wrap yarn around a hardback book.

(2) Using sharp scissors, work along the channel of the book to cut the lengths of yarn free.

(3) Insert a crochet hook from back to front through a stitch along the edge of your work. Fold a length of yarn in half and catch the center with the crochet hook. I like my fringe full, so I use two lengths of yarn.

(4) Pull the hook and yarn through the stitch, creating a loop.

(5) Pass the yarn tails through the loop. Pull the tails firmly to close the loop and secure the fringe to the stitch.

(6) Trim the fringe to an even length.

Optional: Use a garment steamer to relax the fringe before trimming for a uniform look.

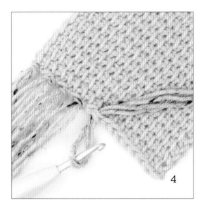

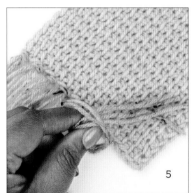

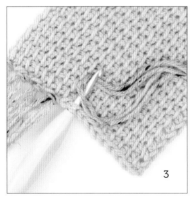

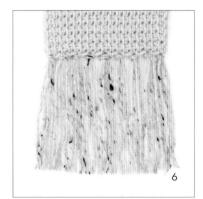

TASSELS

Add a bit of flair to Tunisian crochet housewares and accessories by decorating them with tassels. When laundering projects with tassels, I like to put the piece in a garment bag first. This prevents the tassels from warping or losing their threads.

(1) Wrap yarn around a hardback book.

(2) Cut a long length of yarn. Bring the length of yarn underneath the wrapped threads and tie it securely to the top of the wrap.

(3) Using sharp scissors, work along the channel of the book on the opposite end of the tie to cut the lengths of yarn free.

(4) Tie another length of yarn about 1 inch (2.5 cm) from the top of the tassel. Wrap that piece of yarn around the tassel several times, knot it at the back of the tassel, and use a tapestry needle to thread the tails through the middle of the tassel.

(5) Optional: Repeat step 4 with another length of yarn, working about 1 inch (2.5 cm) down from the previous tie.

(6) Trim the tassel to an even length.

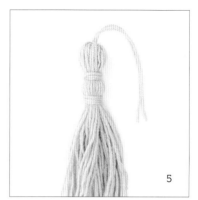

Optional: Use a garment steamer to relax the tassel threads before trimming for a uniform look.

DESIGNS

Juvie Chevron Cowl

If you're anything like me, you start thinking about your next scarf project as soon as you feel the first chill of autumn. This cowl is surprisingly fast and easy to make, so you can start it as soon as the weather turns and finish it in time for chilly fall days.

Fine merino wool yarns make it lightweight and perfect for transitional weather. The chevron pattern is worked using well-placed increases and decreases and features a subtle color sequence. A narrow applied ribbing adds an understated, clean finish.

FINISHED SIZE
10½" (26.5 cm) wide × 54" (137 cm) long before seaming

YARN
Madelinetosh Farm Twist (100% superwash merino wool), category 3—DK weight, 225 yds (206 m)/100 g (3½ oz). *Colors: (A) Paper, 225 yds (206 m), (1 skein); (B) Copper Pink, 60 yds (55 m), (1 skein); (C) Pink Mist Smoke Tree, 60 yds (55 m), (1 skein); (D) Kitten, 60 yds (55 m), (1 skein).*

HOOKS
Size US J/10 (6 mm) Tunisian crochet hook with a 16-inch (40.5-cm) cord
Size US H/8 (5 mm) crochet hook
Or size needed to obtain gauge

NOTIONS
Tapestry needle

GAUGE
11 rows = 4" (10 cm) with Tunisian crochet hook in chevron stitch, unblocked

STITCHES AND TECHNIQUES
- Chevron stitch pattern
- Increasing
- Decreasing
- Changing colors (stripes)
- Mattress stitch seam
- Whipstitch seam
- Applied ribbing technique

NOTE
Find on page 46 a photo tutorial of the applied ribbing technique used in the border.

DIRECTIONS

ROW 1: With A and Tunisian crochet hook, ch 36, pull up a loop in the 2nd ch from hook and each ch across row, RetP. (36 sts)

ROW 2: Yo, *tss 6, tss2tog twice, tss 6 **, yo, tss 2, yo; rep from * across row, ending last rep at **, yo, Lts, RetP.

ROWS 3-147: Rep Row 2 using the following color sequence (colors are changed when 2 loops remain at the end of the RetP—complete the next FwdP and RetP with the new color):

- Complete the following 7 times.
  - B—5 rows
  - A—2 rows
- Complete the following 7 times.
  - C—5 rows
  - A—2 rows
- Complete the following 6 times.
  - D—5 rows
  - A—2 rows
  - D—5 rows

Sl st bind off loosely with D after last row. Fasten off leaving a long tail for seaming.

ASSEMBLY AND FINISHING

Weave in all ends except the last long tail.

Block to 8" (20 cm) wide × 54" (137 cm) long.

Use remaining long tail to mattress seam the bind-off edge to the foundation row.

1. Single crochet in row ends

BORDER

STEP 1: Hold cowl with RS facing you. With A and standard crochet hook, join with a sl st into any row edge stitch near the seam. Ch 1, sc in same st as join, sc in each row edge st around, join with a sl st in the first sc of the round. (**Photo 1**)

STEP 2: Ch 6, sc in 2nd ch from hook and each ch across row, sl st in the sc at the base of the ch and the next sc from step 1, turn. (5 sc)

STEP 3: Sk 2 sl sts, sc BLO across row, turn.

STEP 4: Ch 1, sc BLO across row, sl st in next 2 sc from step 1, turn.

STEP 5: Sk 2 sl sts, sc BLO across row, turn.

STEP 6: Rep steps 4 and 5 around the side of the cowl. When complete, fasten off leaving a tail for seaming. Use the tail to whipstitch the two ends of the border together.

STEP 7: Rep steps 1-6 for the other edge of the cowl. Finish by weaving in any remaining ends.

Kensington Tote Bag

The "dipped" color-block look is one of my favorite techniques for adding minimalist style without having to do complicated colorwork. This tote is made using the Tunisian knit stitch. It looks just like knitting, but it has a sturdier build that will stand up to whatever you need to tote around.

This bag works up quicker than you'd think. It's made in just one piece using a large hook and super bulky wool-blend yarn. Bring it along for trips to the farmers' market or use it to securely hold your laptop when working on the go.

FINISHED SIZE
13½" (34 cm) wide × 15" (38 cm) tall

YARN
Lion Brand Wool-Ease® Thick & Quick (80% acrylic, 20% wool), category 6—super bulky weight, 106 yds (97 m)/170 g (6 oz). *Colors: (A) #116E Succulent, 85 yds (78 m), (1 skein); (B) #099 Fisherman, 175 yds (160 m), (2 skeins).*

HOOK
Size US 12 mm Tunisian crochet hook with 16-inch (40.5-cm) cord
Or size needed to obtain gauge

NOTIONS
Tapestry needle

GAUGE
7 sts and 9 rows = 4" (10 cm) in Tunisian knit stitch, unblocked

STITCHES AND TECHNIQUES
• Tunisian knit stitch
• Changing colors (stripes)
• Adding length in Tunisian crochet
• Picking up stitches
• Mattress stitch seam

through next 2 loops on hook) 7 times. Fasten off and weave in the resulting end. (**Photo 2**) Adjust hook to work remaining loops on hook. Yo with B, ch 1, complete RetP for remaining loops on hook. (**Photo 3**) (2 sets of 8 sts)

ROW 30: Tks 6, Lts, working in the back bump of one of the 12 ch lengths made before, pull up a loop in each of the 12 chs (**Photo 4**), tks 7on the remaining unworked sts, Lts (**Photo 5**), RetP. (28 sts)

ROW 31: Tks across row to last st, Lts, RetP.

ROW 32: Rep Row 31. Sl st bind off loosely, inserting hook into each st as for tks.

SIDE 2

ROW 1: With the RS facing up, rotate Side 1 to work into the foundation stitches. With A, pull up a loop in the base of each ch along the foundation row, RetP (**Photo 6**). (25 sts)

ROWS 2–32: Rep Rows 2–32 of Side 1.

ASSEMBLY AND FINISHING

Weave in all ends.
Steam block flat to 13½" (34 cm) wide × 30" (76 cm) long.
Fold bag in half so the handles are aligned and the RS is facing out. Mattress seam both sides of bag closed using like colors. Weave in any remaining ends.

DIRECTIONS

With B, ch 12. Fasten off and set aside. Rep these instructions so there are 2 sets of 12 chs.

SIDE 1

ROW 1: With A, ch 25, pull up a loop in the 2nd ch from hook and each ch across row, RetP. (25 sts)

ROW 2: Tks across row to last st, Lts, RetP.

ROWS 3–10: Rep Row 2. Cc to B after RetP of last row.

ROWS 11–28: Rep Row 2 with B.

ROW 29: Tks 8, (pull up a loop in the next st as for tks, pull through loop on hook for sl st) 9 times (**Photo 1**), tks 6, Lts, ch 1, (yo, pull

1. Mid-row tks bind off

2. Fastened off left set of stitches

3. Finished Row 29

4. Pulling up loops in ch-12

5. Completing Row 30 forward pass

6. Pulling up loops in the base of Side 1

Hudson Tassel Throw

Any finished project looks instantly more luxurious when it's adorned with plush tassels. Pair them with a textured yet lightweight stitch, and you've got a blanket that's totally Insta-ready.

The generous dimensions and beautiful drape make this the perfect throw for the sofa or the bed, but it would look equally at home wrapped around you at a bonfire. The honeycomb stitch is so addictive, you'll have it completed in no time. Once you finish your first one, you'll be making another—guaranteed!

FINISHED SIZE
42" (106.5 cm) wide × 55" (140 cm/1.4 m) long, not including tassels

YARN
Berroco Vintage Chunky (52% acrylic, 40% wool, 8% nylon), category 5—bulky weight, 136 yds (124 m)/100 g (3½ oz). Color: #6105 Oats, 1485 yds (1358 m) without tassels (11 skeins) or 1720 yds (1573 m) with tassels (13 skeins).

HOOK
Size US L/11 (8 mm) Tunisian crochet hook with 32-inch (81-cm) cord
Or size needed to obtain gauge

NOTIONS
Tapestry needle
8" (20 cm) piece of cardboard, book, or other tassel-making tool

GAUGE
16 sts and 12 rows = 5" (13 cm) in honeycomb stitch, unblocked

STITCHES AND TECHNIQUES
• Honeycomb stitch pattern
• Adding tassels to Tunisian crochet

DIRECTIONS

ROW 1: Ch 124, pull up a loop in the 2nd ch from hook and each ch across row, RetP. (124 sts)

ROW 2: (Tss 1, tps 1) across row to last st, Lts, RetP.

ROW 3: (Tps 1, tss 1) across row to last st, Lts, RetP.

ROWS 4–131: Rep Rows 2 and 3. Sl st bind off loosely after last row. Fasten off and weave in any ends.

EMBELLISHMENTS AND FINISHING

Make twelve 8-inch (20-cm) chunky tassels, wrapping yarn sixty times, as shown in the Embellishments section (see page 69). Evenly space six tassels along each of the blanket's short ends. Use tassel ties to attach the tassels to the blanket's foundation chain and bind-off edge. Weave in ends to WS of work. (**Photos 1 and 2**)

Block to finished dimensions.

1. Knotting tassel to foundation edge

2. Weaving in tassel ends

Empire Tea Towels

There's nothing like a new set of tea towels to brighten up a space. Use these oversize cotton towels for anything from drying flatware to covering fresh-baked rolls and desserts.

The samples I made use a subtle tonal stripe motif, but you can play around with other color combinations to make them your own. This project is portable and works up in no time. Whip up a couple of extras to keep on hand for last-minute gifting.

FINISHED SIZE
14" (35.5 cm) wide × 20" (51 cm) long

YARN
Paintbox Cotton DK (100% cotton), category 3—DK weight, 137 yds (125 m)/50 g (1¾ oz).
Colors: (A) #408 Vanilla Cream, 250 yds (229.5 m), (2 skeins); (B) #455 Peach Orange or #440 Sailor Blue, 35 yds (32 m), (1 skein); (C) #456 Vintage Pink or #411 Royal Blue, 50 yds (46 m), (1 skein).

HOOK
Size US H/8 (5 mm) Tunisian crochet hook with 16-inch (40.5-cm) cord
Or size needed to obtain gauge

NOTIONS
Tapestry needle

GAUGE
22 sts and 16 rows = 4" (10 cm) in lattice stitch, unblocked

STITCHES AND TECHNIQUES
• Lattice stitch pattern
• Changing colors (stripes)

NOTE
The yarn used in this sample was especially elastic and presented a significant difference between the unblocked and blocked length. Substituting yarns in this pattern may impact your finished measurements significantly.

DIRECTIONS

ROW 1: With A, ch 74, pull up a loop in the 2nd ch from hook and each ch across row, RetP. (74 sts)

ROW 2: (Tss2tog, tss first st of tss2tog) across row to last st, Lts, RetP.

ROW 3: Tss 1, (tss2tog, tss first st of tss2tog) across to last 2 sts, tss 1, Lts, RetP.

ROWS 4-63: Rep Rows 2 and 3 using the following color sequence (colors are changed when 2 loops remain at the end of the RetP—complete the FwdP and RetP with the new color):

- A—3 rows
- B—3 rows
- A—4 rows
- C—5 rows
- A—27 rows
- C—5 rows
- A—4 rows
- B—3 rows
- A—6 rows

Sl st bind off loosely with A after last row. Do not fasten off.

HANGING LOOP

ROW 1: Ch 8, sl st in next 3 sts along left edge. (**Photos 1 and 2**). Fasten off.

FINISHING

Weave in all ends and block to finished dimensions.

1. Chain 8 for loop

2. Slip stitch along left edge

Oxford Floor Pouf

Indulge in a lush and lavish floor pouf made in soft, luxurious velvet yarn. This densely stuffed pouf features lots of nubby texture and reverse single crochet "piping" at the edges for a classic look.

Keep your pouf by the couch or your favorite chair to use as a footrest. These cushions also make a comfy seat when you're watching movies from the floor. Better yet, make a collection in coordinating colors and pile them into the corner for a cozy reading nook.

FINISHED SIZE
15" (38 cm) wide × 17" (43 cm) long × 6" (15 cm) deep

YARN
Bernat Velvet (100% polyester), category 5—bulky weight, 315 yds (288 m)/300 g (10½ oz). *Colors: Sample 1 in #2013 Quiet Pink, 625 yds (571.5 m), (2 skeins) and Sample 2 in #2001 Vapor Gray, 625 yds (571.5 m), (2 skeins).*

HOOK
Size US I/9 (5.5 mm) Tunisian crochet hook with 16-inch (40.5-cm) and 32-inch (81-cm) cord
Or size needed to obtain gauge

NOTIONS
High-density foam chair pads measuring 15" (38 cm) × 17" (43 cm) × 3" (7.5 cm), two pads for each cushion
Clear fabric glue
Tapestry needle

GAUGE
14 sts and 10 rows = 4" (10 cm) in seed stitch, unblocked

STITCHES AND TECHNIQUES
• Seed stitch
• Whipstitch seam
• Single crochet seam
• Reverse single crochet

NOTES
• Achieving and maintaining tension while working with velvet yarn can be tricky. Go slowly and count your stitches periodically.
• The finished Top pieces will look too small compared with the foam insert. Don't worry—velvet has great stretch. The finished piece will be taut and smooth over the insert.

DIRECTIONS

TOP (MAKE 2)

ROW 1: With Tunisian crochet hook and 16-inch (40.5-cm) cord, ch 44, pull up a loop in the 2nd ch from hook and each ch across row, RetP. (44 sts)

ROW 2: (Tks 1, tps 1) across row to last st, Lts, RetP.

ROW 3: (Tps 1, tks 1) across row to last st, Lts, RetP.

ROWS 4-37: Rep Rows 2 and 3. Sl st bind off loosely after last row. Fasten off.

SIDE

ROW 1: With Tunisian crochet hook and 32" (81 cm) cord, ch 188, pull up a loop in the 2nd ch from hook and each ch across row, RetP. (188 sts)

ROW 2: (Tks 1, tps 1) across row to last st, Lts, RetP.

ROW 3: (Tps 1, tks 1) across row to last st, Lts, RetP.

ROWS 4-13: Rep Rows 2 and 3. Sl st bind off loosely after last row. Fasten off leaving a tail for seaming.

Use tail to whipstitch seam the short sides of the Side together. Weave in ends.

ASSEMBLY AND FINISHING

Use clear fabric glue to adhere the foam pads to one another. The finished dimensions should be 15" (38 cm) wide × 17" (43 cm) long × 6" (15 cm) deep. Let dry completely.

Lay one Top on top of the foam insert. Wrap Side around the foam insert lengthwise. Use locking stitch markers to attach the corners of the Top to their corresponding stitches on the Side. Due to the varying gauge of velvet, it is easier to eyeball this rather than to try counting stitches.

Remove the foam insert. Sc seam all four edges of Top and Side together, making sure to work through both thicknesses of fabric. Sl st in the first sc of the round. Do not fasten off.

Ch 1, reverse sc in each st around. Sl st in the first sc of the round. Fasten off.

Place the foam insert inside of the pouf. Lay the remaining Top on the foam insert. Use locking stitch markers to attach the corners of the Top to their corresponding stitches on the Side. Remove the foam insert. Sc seam two edges of the Top and Side together. Place the foam insert inside the pouf. Sc seam the remaining 2 edges of the Top and Side together. Sl st in the first sc of the round. Do not fasten off.

Ch 1, reverse sc in each st around. Sl st in the first sc of the round. Fasten off.

Weave in any remaining ends.

Nisa Poncho

Envelop yourself in the moods and colors of fall when you cozy up in your new favorite color-blocked poncho. Worked in an overall openwork pattern using a baby alpaca–blend yarn, it keeps in just the right amount of heat on those crisp, sunny days.

Layer your poncho over any casual outfit for a subtly chic look. Wear it loose for a carefree bohemian style. In the mood for elegant? A wide belt around your poncho adds drama in all the right places. With so many ways to dress up one piece, you'll never want to take it off.

FINISHED SIZES
S/M (L/XL, 2XL/3XL)

FINISHED MEASUREMENTS
35 (39, 43)" [89 (99, 109) cm] wide × 30 (31, 32)" [76 (79, 81) cm] long
Measurements taken with garment lying flat after finishing.

YARN
LB Collection® Chainette (70% baby alpaca, 18% virgin wool, 12% polyamide), category 4—worsted weight, 131 yds (120 m)/50 g (1¾ oz). *Colors: (A) #186 Amber, 750 (865, 985) yds [686 (791, 900.5) m], [6 (7, 8) balls]; (B) #123 Beige, 730 (840, 960) yds [667.5 (768, 877) m], [6 (7, 8) balls].*

HOOK
Size US L/11 (8 mm) Tunisian crochet hook with 32-inch (81-cm) cord
Or size needed to obtain gauge

NOTIONS
Tapestry needle

GAUGE
11 sts and 10 rows = 4" (10 cm) in arrowhead stitch, unblocked

STITCHES AND TECHNIQUES
• Arrowhead stitch pattern
• Changing colors (stripes)
• Slip stitch seam
• Whipstitch seam

NOTES

- Pattern is written for S/M size with additional sizes in parentheses. For some sections, instructions for the different sizes are written separately. Only follow instructions for the size you are making.
- The poncho is made from two panels: the first panel forms the left side and the second panel forms the right side of the garment.
- Adjust the length of the poncho by beginning with a starting chain in any even number.
- Adjust the width of the poncho by changing the number of rows. Complete the foundation row and an even number of rows in pattern stitch.
- The finished poncho is reversible and can be worn with the right side facing out or the wrong side facing out.

DIRECTIONS

PONCHO PANEL (MAKE 2)

ROW 1: With A, ch 168 (174, 178), pull up a loop in the 2nd ch from hook and each ch across row, RetP. [168 (174, 178) sts]

ROW 2: (Tss2tog, yo) across row to last st, Lts, RetP.

ROW 3: (Tss the next st, tks the yo) across row to last st, Lts, RetP.

SIZE S/M ONLY

ROWS 4–42: Rep Rows 2 and 3 using the following color sequence (colors are changed when 2 loops remain at the end of the RetP—complete the FwdP and RetP with the new color):
- A—10 rows
- B—8 rows
- A—8 row
- B—13 rows

SIZE L/XL ONLY

ROWS 4–48: Rep Rows 2 and 3 using the following color sequence (colors are changed when 2 loops remain at the end of the RetP—complete the FwdP and RetP with the new color):
- A—12 rows
- B—9 rows
- A—9 row
- B—15 rows

SIZE 2XL/3XL ONLY

ROWS 4–52: Rep Rows 2 and 3 using the following color sequence (colors are changed when 2 loops remain at the end of the RetP—complete the FwdP and RetP with the new color):
- A—14 rows
- B—9 rows
- A—9 row
- B—17 rows

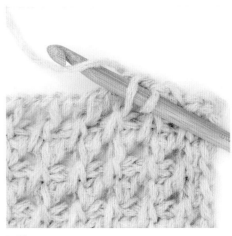

1. Sl st in tss

2. Sl st in yo space

BIND OFF

Continuing with B, (sl st in the vertical bar of the next tss, sl st in the space of the next yarn over) across row to last st, sl st in last st, inserting as for Lts (**Photos 1 and 2**). Fasten off.

ASSEMBLY AND FINISHING

Lay pieces flat next to each other with RS facing up and bind-off edges touching. With B, slip stitch seam the two panels together for 84 (87, 89) stitches to form the center back seam. Fasten off.

Fold piece widthwise with WS facing out. The fold is the shoulder line when worn. Using A, whipstitch seam one side together from the bottom edge toward the fold until 8 (8½, 9)" [20 (21.5, 23) cm] remains before the fold. This creates the armhole. Repeat for the other side.

Weave in any remaining ends and block to finished measurements.

Alpha Wall Hanging

Give me an A! Or a B, or C . . . This wall hanging pattern offers you a whole appliqué alphabet to choose from. Welcome baby in a big way, add some cheer to a child's room, or decorate a dorm with this fun, customizable project.

Start your wall hanging by crocheting a rectangle in Tunisian simple stitch, then add textured embellishments like cross stitch, pom-poms, and playful fringe. A wooden dowel and hanging loop finish things off so you can display your new art in your sweetest spaces.

FINISHED SIZE
8½" (21.5 cm) wide × 12" (30.5 cm) long, not including fringe; 20" (51 cm) long, including fringe)

YARN
WeCrochet Wool of the Andes (100% Peruvian highland wool), category 4—worsted weight, 110 yds (110.5 m)/50 g (2 oz). *Colors: (A) Cloud, 95 yds (87 m), (1 ball); (B) Blossom Heather, 50 yds (46 m), (1 ball); (C) Cobblestone Heather, 40 yds (36.5 m), (1 ball); (D) Pumpkin, 40 yds (36.5 m), (1 ball).*

HOOK
Size US J/10 (6 mm) Tunisian crochet hook with 8-inch (20-cm) cord
Or size needed to obtain gauge

NOTIONS
⅜-inch (1-cm) diameter × 12-inch (30.5-cm) long wooden dowel
1⅝-inch (4-cm) Clover pom-pom maker (yellow) or other pom-pom making supplies
Tapestry needle

GAUGE
15 sts and 12½ rows = 4" (10 cm) in Tunisian simple stitch, unblocked

STITCHES AND TECHNIQUES
- Tunisian simple stitch
- Cross stitch on Tunisian crochet
- Adding embellishments to Tunisian crochet including pom-poms and fringe

NOTE
When choosing colors for your letter and using a light-colored background like I did here, use your lightest color for the main letter, the darkest color for the outline, and the mid-tone color for the shadow. This will ensure that you have strong contrast and your chosen initial stands out from the background.

DIRECTIONS

BACKGROUND

ROW 1: With A, ch 33, pull up a loop in the 2nd ch from hook and each ch across row, RetP. (33 sts)

ROWS 2–38: Tss across row to last st, Lts, RetP. Sl st bind off loosely after last row. Fasten off. Steam block to 8½" (21.5 cm) wide × 12" (30.5 cm) long.

Using the chart on the opposite page, add cross stitch letter to right side of background, leaving a five-stitch margin along the left and right sides, a five-row margin along the top, and an eight-row margin along the bottom. Weave in the ends.

EMBELLISHMENTS AND FINISHING

Thread a 24-inch (61-cm) length of color A onto a tapestry needle. Begin wrapping the yarn around the dowel, picking up one stitch from the bind-off edge on each wrap. Secure the ends and weave them in.

Cut an 18-inch (46-cm) length of color A. Tie to either end of the dowel to create the hanger.

Cut several 16-inch (40.5-cm) lengths of colors B, C, and D. Holding yarn lengths double, attach yarn as fringe to hang from the foundation chain. Steam the fringe lightly to relax the fibers and trim as needed. **(Photo 1)**

Make five pom-poms in the colors of your choice using the Clover pom-pom maker. Evenly space them along the foundation row of the background. Insert the tails of the pom-poms into the stitches of the foundation row and tie firmly to the back of the work. Weave in the ends. **(Photo 2)**

Weave in any remaining ends.

1. Attaching the fringe

2. Attaching the pom-poms

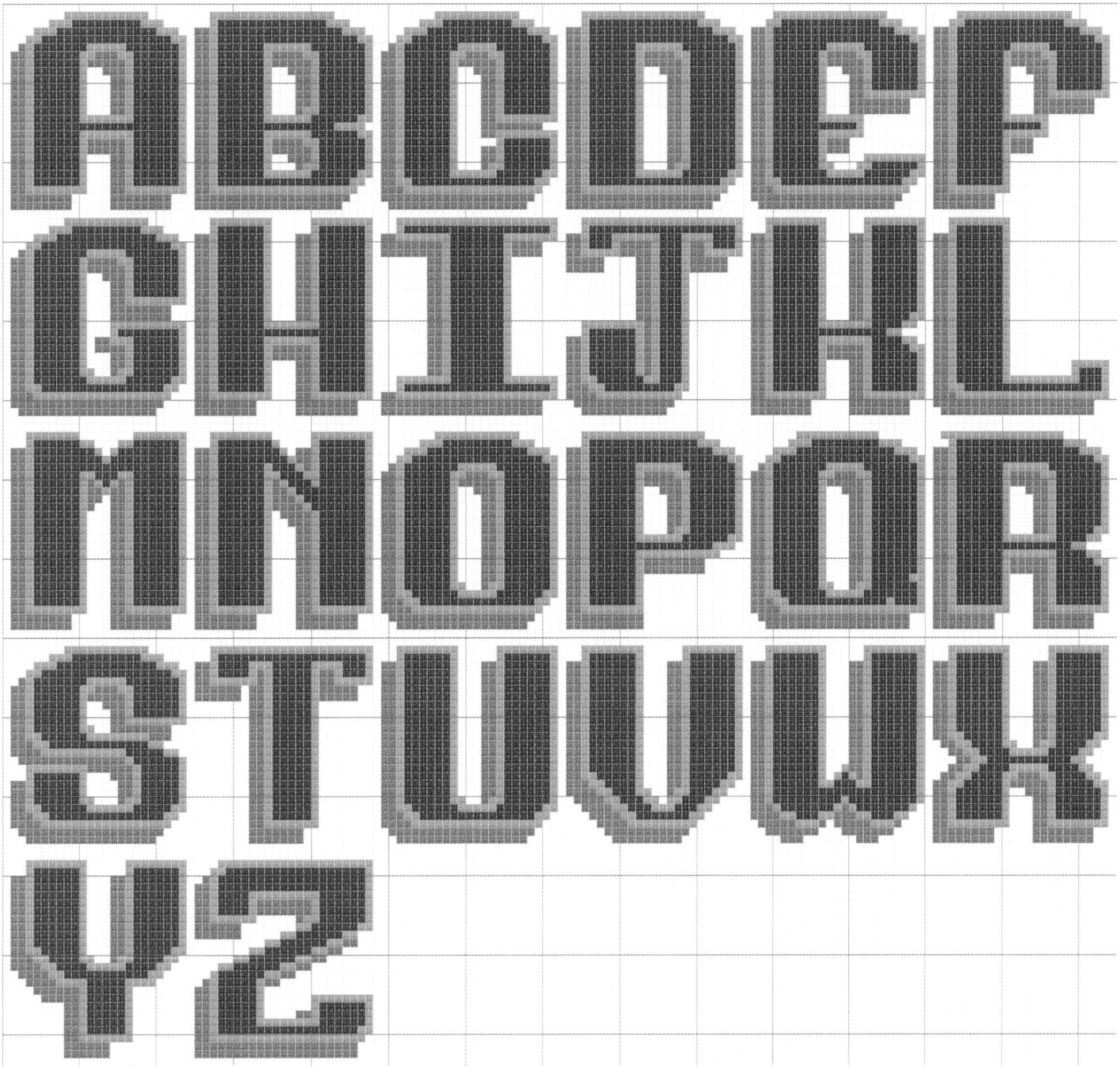
ABCDEF
GHIJKL
MNOPQR
STUVWX
YZ

Midway Fringe Scarf

A colorful, versatile scarf is the one accessory every trendsetter needs when building a capsule wardrobe. Soft and fine in silk/mohair and merino/cashmere yarns, this extra-long rectangle scarf is easy to customize and offers infinite styling options.

The color shift pattern is inspired by classic collegiate fashion, while the strand of mohair running throughout keeps it ethereal and light. Unisex by design, this scarf makes a great gift for the trendy guy or gal on your gift list.

FINISHED SIZE
12" (30.5 cm) wide × 81" (206 cm) long, not including fringe

YARN
WeCrochet Aloft (72% super kid mohair, 28% silk), category 0—lace weight, 260 yds (238 m)/25 g (1 oz). *Color: (A) White, 655 yds (599 m), (3 balls).*
WeCrochet Capra DK (85% merino wool, 15% cashmere), category 3—DK weight, 123 yds (112.5 m)/50 g (1½ oz). *Colors: (B) Adriatic Heather, 240 yds (219.5 m), (2 balls); (C) Moonstone Heather, 200 yds (183 m), (2 balls); (D) Tansy Heather, 240 yds (219.5 m), (2 balls).*

HOOK
Size US J/10 (6 mm) Tunisian crochet hook with 16-inch (40.5-cm) cord
Or size needed to obtain gauge

NOTIONS
7-inch (18-cm) piece of cardboard or other supplies to make fringe
Tapestry needle

GAUGE
17 sts = 5" (13 cm) in extended Tunisian simple stitch, unblocked
10 rows = 5½" (14 cm) in extended Tunisian simple stitch, unblocked

STITCHES AND TECHNIQUES
• Extended Tunisian simple stitch
• Changing colors (two-tone stripes)
• Adding embellishments to Tunisian crochet, including fringe

1. Inserting hook into first chain after the last st

2. Pulling up the loop in the first chain after the last st

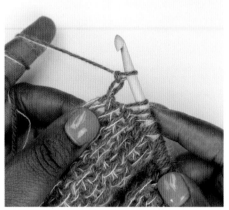

3. Chain 1 after loop complete. Chain 1 of RetP made.

NOTES

- A strand of A is carried together with the accent colors throughout this pattern. Carry a separate strand of A when changing between accent colors in Sections 2 and 3.
- To work the last stitch of the etss, pull up a loop in the first ch after the last stitch of the previous row, followed by a ch-1. The last stitch of the next etss row will be worked in this chain. The return pass (RetP) is worked as normal (**Photos 1–3**).

DIRECTIONS

SECTION 1

ROW 1: Holding 1 strand of A tog throughout, with B, ch 44, (pull up a loop, ch 1) in the 3rd ch from hook and in each ch across the row, RetP. (43 sts)

ROW 2: Ch 1, etss in each st across row to last st, pull up a loop in the last ch-1 made on the FwdP of the previous row, ch 1, RetP.

ROWS 3–36: Rep Row 2.

SECTION 2

ROW 1: Continuing with B and holding a strand of A throughout, ch 1, etss in each st across to last st, pull up a loop in the last ch-1 made on the FwdP of the previous row, ch 1, drop B, cc to C, RetP.

ROW 2: Ch 1, etss in each st across row to last st, pull up a loop in the last ch-1 made on the FwdP of the previous row, ch 1, drop C, cc to B, RetP.

ROWS 3–35: Rep Rows 1 and 2, ending with a repeat of Row 1.

ROW 36: Ch 1, etss in each st across row to last st, pull up a loop in the last ch-1 made on the FwdP of the previous row, ch 1, drop C, cc to B, RetP, cc to D in last yo. Fasten off B.

SECTION 3

ROW 1: Continuing with D and holding a strand of A throughout, ch 1, etss in each st across to last st, pull up a loop in the last ch-1 made on the FwdP of the previous row, ch 1, drop D, cc to C, RetP.

ROW 2: Ch 1, etss in each st across row to last st, pull up a loop in the last ch-1 made on the FwdP of the previous row, ch 1, drop C, cc to D, RetP.

ROWS 3–35: Rep Rows 1 and 2, ending with a repeat of Row 1.

ROW 36: Ch 1, etss in each st across row to last st, pull up a loop in the last ch-1 made on the FwdP of the previous row, ch 1, drop C, cc to D, RetP. Fasten off C.

SECTION 4

ROW 1: Continuing with D and holding a strand of A throughout, ch 1, etss in each st across row to last st, pull up a loop in the last ch-1 made on the FwdP of the previous row, ch 1, RetP.

ROWS 2–36: Rep Row 1.
Sl st bind off loosely after last row. Fasten off.

EMBELLISHMENTS AND FINISHING

Weave in all ends.
Steam block scarf to 12" (30.5 cm) wide × 81" (206 cm) long.
Hold one strand of A with one strand of C and make 14-inch (35-cm) long strands of yarn for fringe using the 7-inch (18-cm) piece of cardboard.

Holding two strands of A and two strands of C together, add fringe to every other stitch along the foundation and bind-off edges—22 fringe groups along each edge. Steam and trim the fringe as needed.

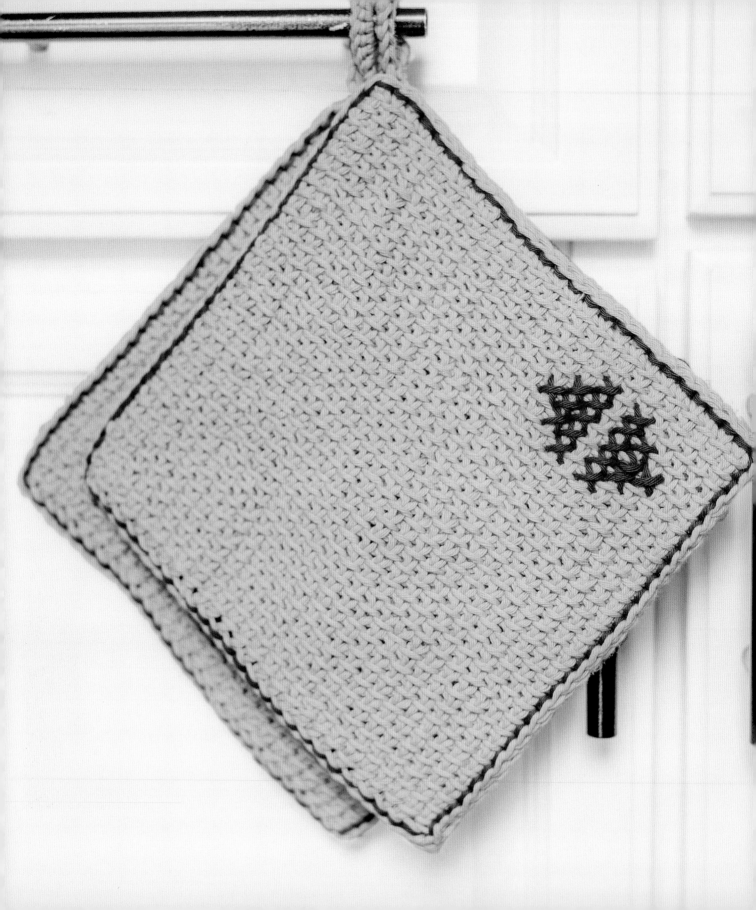

Geo Pot Holders

These pot holders are so pretty, it would be a crime not to display them. In addition to the nubby fabric, geometric cross-stitch accents, and backstitch detail, they also feature a handy hanging loop in the top corner.

Made double-thick for added insulation, these hot pads make a charming bridal or holiday gift when paired with a bestselling cookbook and your favorite spices. The design and color possibilities are endless, so mix and match to your heart's content.

FINISHED SIZE
8" (20 cm) wide × 8" (20 cm) long

YARN
Paintbox Cotton Aran (100% cotton), category 4—heavy worsted/Aran weight, 93 yds (85 m)/50 g (1¾ oz). *Colors: (A) #608 Vanilla Cream, 115 yds (105 m), (2 skeins); (B) Accent Color, #656 Vintage Pink and #606 Slate Grey, 15 yds (14 m) each, (1 skein each).*

HOOK
Size US I/9 (5.5 mm) Tunisian crochet hook with 4-inch (10-cm) cord
Or size needed to obtain gauge

NOTIONS
Tapestry needle

GAUGE
12 sts and 10 rows = 3" (7.5 cm) in Tunisian simple stitch, unblocked

STITCHES AND TECHNIQUES
- Tunisian simple stitch
- Single crochet
- Backstitch seam
- Cross stitch on Tunisian crochet

NOTE
Each hot pad is made with the same Tunisian simple stitch pattern. Choose a cross stitch pattern to add to the front from the suggested designs, or get creative and design your own 7 × 7 stitch pattern.

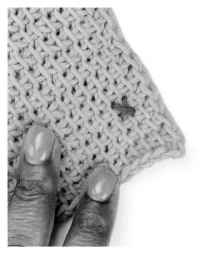

1. Placement of bottom right stitch of cross stitch

2. Loop, Row 1

3. Loop, Row 2

DIRECTIONS

FRONT

ROW 1: With A, ch 30, pull up a loop in the 2nd ch from hook and each ch across row, RetP. (30 sts)

ROWS 2-26: Tss across row to last st, Lts, RetP. Sl st bind off loosely after last row. Fasten off.

Add cross stitch accent in B to Front. Bottom right stitch of chart corresponds to the 3rd stitch of the 4th row on Front (**Photo 1**). Weave in ends.

CROSS STITCH MOTIFS

Add unique style to your hot pads by stitching on the front one of these minimalist designs (shown at right).

BACK

Repeat Rows 1-26 of Front. Do not fasten off.

HANGING LOOP

ROW 1: Ch 8, sl st in last st of bind off row to form a loop, turn. (**Photo 2**)

ROW 2: Ch 1, 15 sc in the loop (**Photo 3**), sl st in last st of bind off row. Fasten off. Weave in ends.

ASSEMBLY AND FINISHING

Weave in the remaining ends and lightly steam block pieces to finished dimensions.

Align Front and Back together with right sides facing out. With B and tapestry needle, beginning on the bottom edge of the square, backstitch around the square to seam all four sides together.

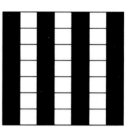

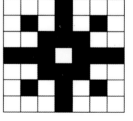

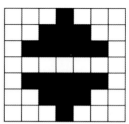

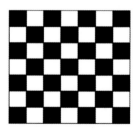

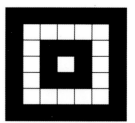

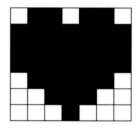

Elm Slouch Hat

Can you believe this beanie isn't knit?! With clean lines and intentional design, this piece is bound to look great on anyone. You better make more than one—I'm sure someone in your family is going to want to "borrow" it. *wink wink*

The sleek color-dipped style is made using a stunning yak/wool blend yarn that's toasty warm and oh so soft. The extra-wide ribbed brim keeps your hat firmly in place. Fold the brim for the classic beanie style or keep it unfolded for that cool slouchy look.

FINISHED SIZE
8½" (21.5 cm) wide × 9" (23 cm) tall when lying flat after seaming, sized to fit head circumference 20–22" (51–56 cm)

YARN
The Yarn Collective Hudson Worsted (85% merino wool, 15% yak), category 4—worsted weight, 197 yds (180 m)/100 g (3½ oz). *Colors: (A) #401 Natural, 120 yds (110 m), (1 skein); (B) #406 Pumpkin, 50 yds (46 m), (1 skein).*

HOOKS
Size US J/10 (6 mm) Tunisian crochet hook with 16-inch (40.5-cm) cord
Or size needed to obtain gauge
Size US 7 (4.5 mm) crochet hook

NOTIONS
One faux leather tag (optional)
Tapestry needle

GAUGE
16 sts and 14 rows = 4" (10 cm) with the Tunisian crochet hook in Tunisian knit stitch, unblocked

STITCHES AND TECHNIQUES
- Tunisian knit stitch
- Single crochet in back loop only
- Picking up stitches
- Changing colors (stripes)
- Decreasing
- Mattress stitch seam

NOTES
- Decrease (*dec*): Insert hook into next stitch as for tss, insert hook into next stitch as for tks, yo, pull up a loop in the 2 stitches. (**Photos 1 and 2**, page 124)
- This pattern can easily be made in the round, but it is made flat here to keep it beginner-friendly.

1. Inserting hook for tks dec

2. Pulling up the loop after the tks dec

DIRECTIONS

RIBBING

ROW 1: With A and the standard crochet hook, ch 13, sc in 2nd ch from hook and each st across row, turn. (12 sc)

ROW 2: Ch 1, sc BLO across row, turn.

ROWS 3–70: Rep Row 2.
Rotate ribbing to work along row ends.

BODY

ROW 1: With Tunisian crochet hook, sk first row, pull up a loop in the end of each remaining row across ribbing, RetP. (70 sts)

ROW 2: Tks across row to last st, Lts, RetP.

ROWS 3–12: Rep Row 2, cc to B after last row. Fasten off A leaving a long tail for seaming.

ROWS 13–17: Rep Row 2.

ROW 18: (Dec over next 2 sts, tks 5) across row to last 6 sts, dec over next 2 sts, tks 3, Lts, RetP. (60 sts)

ROW 19: Tks across row to last st, Lts, RetP.

ROW 20: (Dec over next 2 sts, tks 4) across row to last 5 sts, dec over next 2 sts, tks 2, Lts, RetP. (50 sts).

ROW 21: Tks across row to last st, Lts, RetP.

ROW 22: (Dec over next 2 sts, tks 3) across row to last 4 sts, dec over next 2 sts, tks 1, Lts, RetP. (40 sts)

ROW 23: Tks across row to last st, Lts, RetP.

ROW 24: (Dec over next 2 sts, tks 2) across row to last 3 sts, dec over next 2 sts, Lts, RetP. (30 sts)

ROW 25: Tks across row to last st, Lts, RetP.

ROW 26: (Dec over next 2 sts) 2 times, tks 1, (dec over next 2 sts, tks 1) across row to last 3 sts, dec over next 2 sts, Lts, RetP. (20 sts)

ROW 27: Tks across row to last st, Lts, RetP.

ROW 28: (Dec over next 2 sts) across row to last st, Lts, RetP. (11 sts)
Sl st bind off loosely, leaving a long tail for seaming the sides of the B rows of the hat.

ASSEMBLY AND FINISHING

Thread tail through 11 sts at bind off edge. Pull tail to cinch top closed.

Use remainder of tail to mattress seam sides of B rows of hat together. Use tail of A from Row 12 to mattress seam sides of remaining rows together.

Weave in all ends and steam block lightly if needed. Attach the leather tag to ribbing following package directions.

Ashford Striped Pillow

Simple stitches worked on the bias (i.e., diagonally) present the beautiful gradations of hand-dyed yarn in their best light. If you have some partial skeins in your stash that you can't bear to part with, the geometric stripe motif of this throw pillow is a great way to show them off. This is also the perfect project to try specific techniques like striping, increasing, and decreasing.

FINISHED SIZE
16" (40.5 cm) wide × 12" (30.5 cm) long

YARN
Malabrigo Rios (100% superwash merino wool), category 4—worsted weight, 210 yds (192 m)/100 g (3½ oz). *Colors: (A) #RIO208 Camel, 230 yds (210 m), (2 skeins); (B) #RIO150 Azul Profundo, 90 yds (82 m), (1 skein).*

HOOK
Size US J/10 (6 mm) Tunisian crochet hook with 16-inch (40.5-cm) cord
Or size needed to obtain gauge

NOTIONS
16-inch (40.5-cm) × 12-inch (30.5-cm) pillow form
Tapestry needle

GAUGE
16 sts × 15 rows = 4" (10 cm) in Tunisian simple stitch, unblocked

STITCHES AND TECHNIQUES
- Tunisian simple stitch
- Increasing
- Decreasing
- Changing colors (stripes)
- Running stitch seam

DIRECTIONS

STRIPE PATTERN

Complete Side 1 and Side 2 of pillow, changing color as instructed in Stripe Pattern (colors are changed when 2 loops remain at the end of the RetP—complete the FwdP and RetP with the new color):

- A—Rows 1-41
- B—Rows 42-46
- A—Rows 47-51
- B—Rows 52-56
- A—Rows 57-61
- B—Rows 62-71

SIDE 1

ROW 1: With A, ch 3, pull up a loop in the 2nd ch from hook and the remaining ch, RetP. (3 tss)

ROW 2: Yo, tss 1, yo, Lts, RetP. (5 tss)

ROW 3: Yo, tss each st across to last st, yo, Lts, RetP. (7 tss)

ROWS 4-31: Rep Row 3. (63 tss)

ROW 32: Tss2tog, tss each st across to last st, yo, Lts, RetP.

ROWS 33-40: Rep Row 32.

ROW 41: Tss2tog, tss each st across to last 3 sts, tss2tog, Lts, RetP. (61 tss)

ROWS 42-69: Rep Row 41. (5 tss)

ROW 70: Tss2tog over next 2 sts, tss2tog over next st and last st (insert hook under both loops of last st as for Lts), RetP. (3 tss) **(Photo 1)**

ROW 71: Insert hook as for tss in next st, insert hook under both loops of last st, yo, pull through all loops on hook. **(Photos 2 and 3)** Fasten off. Weave in ends.

SIDE 2

ROWS 1-31: Rep Rows 1-31 of Side 1. (63 tss)

ROW 32: Yo, tss each st across to last 3 sts, tss2tog, Lts, RetP.

ROWS 33-40: Rep Row 32.

ROWS 41-71: Rep Rows 41-71 of Side 1.

ASSEMBLY AND FINISHING

Place sides together with WS facing each other and stripes lined up together. Using A and a tapestry needle, seam three sides together using a running stitch. Insert the pillow form. Seam remaining side together with a running stitch. Weave in any remaining ends.

1. Inserting hook as for tss2tog

2. Inserting hook as for Lts

3. Pull through all loops on hook

Sulta Triangle Wrap

Lucky you—you've finally found the one winter staple you can wear with every outfit. This scarf is equal parts squishy and cozy in single-ply Aran-weight yarn with bold statement stripes that complement any winter coat.

Worked in smooth Tunisian full stitch, this is one project you'll never want to put down. The triangle shape emerges through the use of repeated yarn-over increases, giving you a chance to master this shaping technique. Carrying colors up the side of your work when not in use cuts down on weaving in ends later.

FINISHED SIZE
72" (183-cm) wingspan × 22 1/2" (57-cm) depth along center stitch

YARN
We Are Knitters The Petite Wool (100% Peruvian highland wool), category 4—heavy worsted/Aran weight, 153 yds (140 m)/100 g (3 1/2 oz), Colors: (A) Spotted Beige, 300 yds (274 m), (2 balls); (B) Forest Green, 295 yds (270 m), (2 balls).

HOOK
Size US N/15 (10 mm) Tunisian crochet hook with 32-inch (81-cm) cord
Or size needed to obtain gauge

NOTIONS
Stitch marker
Tapestry needle

GAUGE
9 sts × 9 1/2 rows = 4" (10 cm) in Tunisian full stitch, unblocked

STITCHES AND TECHNIQUES
• Tunisian full stitch
• Tunisian knit stitch
• Tunisian simple stitch
• Increasing
• Changing colors (stripes)

NOTES
• Place a locking stitch marker on the center stitch beginning in Row 3. Move the stitch marker up on the forward pass as you go so you can always find the center stitch.
• The finished scarf will still have a bit of curl to it, even after blocking. If you prefer no curl, replace your last two rows with tss, maintaining the increases.

DIRECTIONS

ROW 1: With A, ch 7, pull up a loop in the 2nd ch from hook and each ch across row, RetP. (7 sts)

ROW 2: Tss the next st, yo, tfs in the next 2 sps between sts, tss 1, tfs in the next 2 sps between sts, yo, tss 1, Lts, RetP, cc to B. (11 sts)

ROW 3: Tss the next st, yo, tks the yo (**Photos 1 and 2**), tfs in the space between the yo and the next tss, tfs in the next 2 spaces, tss 1 (this is the center stitch), tfs in the next 2 spaces, tfs in the space between the next st and the yo, tks the yo, yo, tss 1, Lts, RetP. (15 sts)

ROW 4: Tss the next st, yo, tks the yo, tfs in the space between the yo and the next st, tfs in each sp to the center st including the sp before the center st, tss the center st, tfs the sp after the center st, tfs in each sp to the next yo including the sp before the yo, tks the yo, yo, tss 1, Lts, RetP, cc to A. (19 sts)

ROWS 5-52: Rep Row 4 using the following color sequence (colors are changed when 2 loops remain at the end of the RetP—complete the FwdP and RetP with the new color):

(1) Complete the following 10 times:
- A—2 rows
- B—2 rows

(2) A—4 rows

(3) B—3 rows

(4) A—1 row

Sl st bind off loosely with A after last row. Fasten off.

FINISHING

Weave in any remaining ends and block to finished dimensions.

1. Identifying the yo

2. Tks the yo

Cheeky Bath Mat

Could you use a little fun to jazz up your bathroom routine? Ideal for adding a pop of color to small spaces, this bath mat features a cheeky greeting that's crocheted right in using stranded colorwork.

The crisp lines of this bath mat are formed by a washable cotton tube yarn. The yarn also has a nylon core to allow for faster drying and a rounded construction to create a dense, sturdy fabric. Finish it off with a no-slip backing for extra grip.

FINISHED SIZE
30" (76 cm) wide × 19" (48 cm) long

YARN
Bernat Maker Home Dec (72% cotton, 28% nylon), category 5—bulky weight, 317 yds (290 m)/250g (9 oz). *Colors: (A) Aqua, 360 yds (330 m), (2 skeins); (B) Black, 100 yds (91 m), (1 skein).*

HOOK
Size US K/10 1/2 (6.5 mm) Tunisian crochet hook with 24-inch (61-cm) cord
Or size needed to obtain gauge

NOTIONS
Nonslip rug pad
Clear fabric glue
Tapestry needle

GAUGE
14 sts and 10 rows = 4" (10 cm) in Tunisian simple stitch, unblocked

STITCHES AND TECHNIQUES
• Tunisian simple stitch
• Changing colors (stranded colorwork)
• Reading a chart

NOTES
Use the stranded colorwork technique and Tunisian simple stitch to complete the chart. The chart shows the first 43 sts of each row and Rows 1–26. Read the chart from right to left and note that the loop on your hook at the beginning of the FwdP counts as the first square. White squares are worked in color A, and black squares are worked in color B.

DIRECTIONS

ROW 1: With A, ch 95, pull up a loop in the 2nd ch from hook and each ch across row, RetP. (95 sts)

ROWS 2–26: Tss across to last st following the chart for color changes across the first 43 sts and working the remaining sts with A, Lts, RetP. At end of the last row, fasten off B.

ROWS 27–42: With A, tss each st across to last st, Lts, RetP. Sl st bind off loosely after last row. Fasten off. Weave in all ends. With B and RS facing up, pull up a loop under both loops of any stitch along the foundation row. Sl st in each stitch along all four edges of work. Fasten off and weave in any remaining ends. **(Photos 1 and 2)**

FINISHING

Steam block mat to finished dimensions.

Cut the nonslip rug pad to 28" (71 cm) × 15" (38 cm). With WS of mat facing up, center the rug pad in the middle of the mat. Adhere the rug pad to the mat using thin beads of fabric glue. Let the fabric glue dry thoroughly before using. **(Photo 3)**

Optional: Weigh down the rug pad while the glue dries. I used a large piece of cardboard and stacked books on top of it.

1. Beginning the slip-stitch border

2. Slip-stitch border at corner

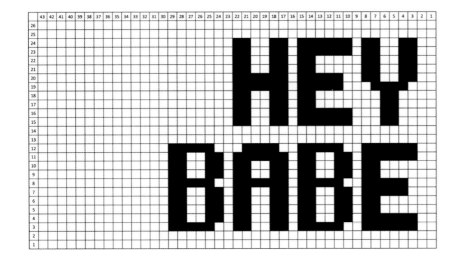

3. Adding the rug pad

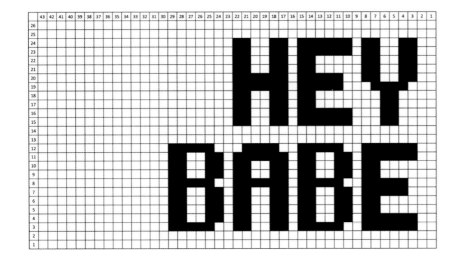

Motley Blanket

The intarsia color-change method lets you create sweeping color blocks of any size and shape. In this throw blanket, intarsia produces a graphic, abstract colorscape that's playful, modern, and inviting.

Simple stitchwork lets strong colors shine, so have fun choosing a palette that complements your personal style. Best of all, this colorwork technique is way easier than you think. Just follow along, row by row, and soon you'll be painting with yarn too.

FINISHED SIZE
48" (122 cm) wide × 58" (147 cm) long

YARN
Berroco Vintage® (52% acrylic, 40% wool, 8% nylon), category 4—worsted weight, 218 yds (199 m)/100 g (3½ oz). *Colors: (A) Navy, 625 yds (571.5 m), (3 skeins); (B) #5106 Smoke, 325 yds (297 m), (2 skeins); (C) #5127 Butternut, 415 yds (379.5 m), (2 skeins); (D) #51180 Grapefruit, 505 yds (462 m), (3 skeins); (E) #5194 Breezeway, 345 yds (315 m), (2 skeins); (F) #5101 Mochi, 145 yds (132.5 m), (1 skein).*

HOOKS
Size US K/10½ (6.5 mm) Tunisian crochet hook with 32-inch (81-cm) cord
Or size needed to obtain gauge
Size US J/10 (6 mm) crochet hook

NOTIONS
Tapestry needle

GAUGE
19 sts and 16 rows = 5" (13 cm) with Tunisian crochet hook in Tunisian simple stitch, unblocked

STITCHES AND TECHNIQUES
• Tunisian simple stitch
• Changing colors (intarsia method)
• Adding a crochet border
• Single crochet in joined rounds

NOTES

- When making this blanket, work all stitches in Tunisian simple stitch and change color as instructed using the intarsia method. The first loop on the hook at the beginning of the FwdP is considered the first stitch in the row and is included in the row instructions. For example, "41 A, 53 C, 83 B" means to work 41 tss in A (counting the first loop on the hook as 1), the next 53 tss in C, and the final 83 tss in B (including the Lts).
- Fasten off colors when they are no longer in use.

DIRECTIONS

BODY

ROW 1: With A and Tunisian crochet hook, ch 177, pull up a loop in the 2nd ch from hook and each ch across row, RetP. (177 st)

ROW 2: Tss across row to last st, Lts, RetP.

ROWS 3-20: Rep Row 2.

ROW 21: 173 A, 4 B, RetP.

ROW 22: 170 A, 7 B, RetP.

ROW 23: 167 A, 10 B, RetP.

ROW 24: 163 A, 14 B, RetP.

ROW 25: 160 A, 17 B, RetP.

ROW 26: 157 A, 20 B, RetP.

ROW 27: 154 A, 23 B, RetP.

ROW 28: 151 A, 26 B, RetP.

ROW 29: 148 A, 29 B, RetP.

ROW 30: 145 A, 32 B, RetP.

ROW 31: 142 A, 35 B, RetP.

ROW 32: 139 A, 38 B, RetP.

ROW 33: 136 A, 41 B, RetP.

ROW 34: 133 A, 44 B, RetP.

ROW 35: 130 A, 47 B, RetP.

ROW 36: 127 A, 50 B, RetP.

ROW 37: 124 A, 53 B, RetP.

ROW 38: 121 A, 56 B, RetP.

ROW 39: 118 A, 59 B, RetP.

ROW 40: 115 A, 62 B, RetP.

ROW 41: 112 A, 65 B, RetP.

ROW 42: 109 A, 68 B, RetP.

ROW 43: 106 A, 71 B, RetP.

ROW 44: 103 A, 74 B, RetP.

ROW 45: 100 A, 77 B, RetP.

ROW 46: 97 A, 80 B, RetP.

ROW 47: 94 A, 83 B, RetP.

ROW 48: 91 A, 86 B, RetP

ROW 49: 88 A, 89 B, RetP.

ROW 50: 85 A, 92 B, RetP.

ROW 51: 82 A, 95 B, RetP.

ROW 52: 79 A, 98 B, RetP.

ROW 53: 76 A, 101 B, RetP.

ROW 54: 73 A, 3 C, 101 B, RetP.

ROW 55: 70 A, 6 C, 101 B, RetP.

ROW 56: 67 A, 11 C, 99 B, RetP.

ROW 57: 64 A, 15 C, 98 B, RetP.

ROW 58: 61 A, 20 C, 96 B, RetP.

ROW 59: 58 A, 25 C, 94 B, RetP.

ROW 60: 55 A, 30 C, 92 B, RetP.

ROW 61: 53 A, 34 C, 90 B, RetP.

ROW 62: 50 A, 38 C, 89 B, RetP.

ROW 63: 47 A, 43 C, 87 B, RetP.

ROW 64: 44 A, 48 C, 85 B, RetP.

ROW 65: 41 A, 53 C, 83 B, RetP.

ROW 66: 38 A, 56 C, 2 D, 81 B, RetP.

ROW 67: 35 A, 59 C, 4 D, 79 B, RetP.

ROW 68: 32 A, 61 C, 7 D, 77 B, RetP.

ROW 69: 29 A, 63 C, 10 D, 75 B, RetP.

ROW 70: 26 A, 65 C, 13 D, 73 B, RetP.

ROW 71: 23 A, 67 C, 16 D, 71 B, RetP.

ROW 72: 21 A, 69 C, 18 D, 69 B, RetP.

ROW 73: 18 A, 70 C, 21 D, 68 B, RetP.

ROW 74: 15 A, 72 C, 24 D, 66 B, RetP.

ROW 75: 12 A, 74 C, 27 D, 64 B, RetP.

ROW 76: 9 A, 77 C, 30 D, 61 B, RetP.

ROW 77: 6 A, 80 C, 32 D, 59 B, RetP.

ROW 78: 3 A, 82 C, 35 D, 57 B, RetP.

ROW 79: 1 A, 83 C, 38 D, 55 B, RetP.

ROW 80: 84 C, 40 D, 53 B, RetP.

ROW 81: 83 C, 43 D, 51 B, RetP.

ROW 82: 82 C, 45 D, 50 B, RetP.

ROW 83: 81 C, 48 D, 48 B, RetP.

ROW 84: 81 C, 50 D, 46 B, RetP.

ROW 85: 80 C, 54 D, 43 B, RetP.

ROW 86: 79 C, 56 D, 42 B, RetP.

ROW 87: 78 C, 59 D, 40 B, RetP.

ROW 88: 78 C, 61 D, 38 B, RetP.

ROW 89: 77 C, 64 D, 36 B, RetP.

ROW 90: 77 C, 66 D, 34 B, RetP.

ROW 91: 76 C, 69 D, 32 B, RetP.

ROW 92: 75 C, 72 D, 30 B, RetP.

ROW 93: 74 C, 75 D, 28 B, RetP.

ROW 94: 74 C, 77 D, 26 B, RetP.

ROW 95: 73 C, 80 D, 24 B, RetP.

ROW 96: 72 C, 83 D, 22 B, RetP.

ROW 97: 71 C, 86 D, 20 B, RetP.

ROW 98: 71 C, 88 D, 18 B, RetP.

ROW 99: 70 C, 91 D, 16 B, RetP.

ROW 100: 69 C, 94 D, 14 B, RetP.

ROW 101: 68 C, 97 D, 12 B, RetP.

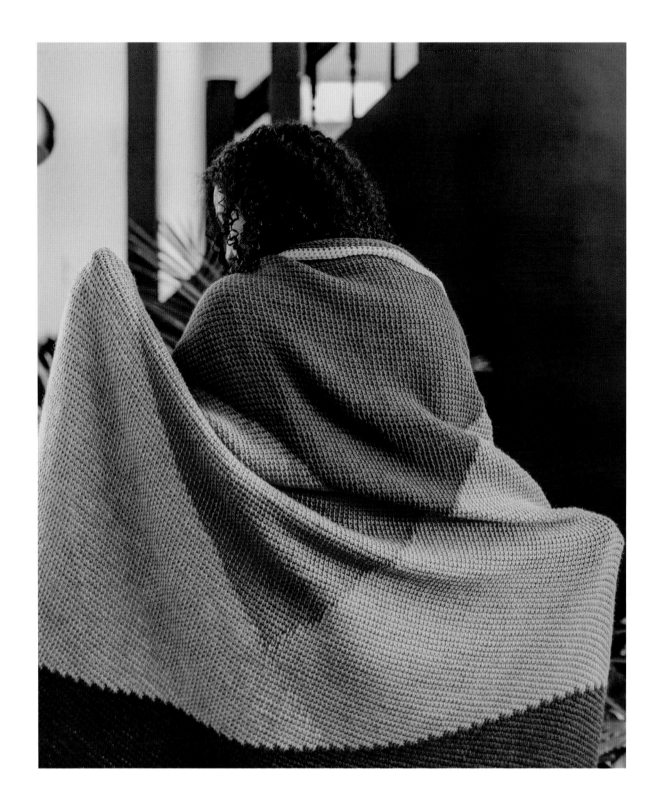

ROW 102: 68 C, 99 D, 10 B, RetP.
ROW 103: 67 C, 102 D, 8 B, RetP.
ROW 104: 66 C, 105 D, 6 B, RetP.
ROW 105: 65 C, 2 E, 105 D, 5 B, RetP.
ROW 106: 64 C, 4 E, 105 D, 4 B, RetP.
ROW 107: 64 C, 5 E, 105 D, 3 B, RetP.
ROW 108: 63 C, 7 E, 106 D, 1 B, RetP.
ROW 109: 62 C, 9 E, 106 D, RetP.
ROW 110: 61 C, 10 E, 106 D, RetP.
ROW 111: 61 C, 11 E, 105 D, RetP.
ROW 112: 60 C, 13 E, 104 D, RetP.
ROW 113: 59 C, 15 E, 103 D, RetP.
ROW 114: 58 C, 17 E, 102 D, RetP.
ROW 115: 58 C, 18 E, 101 D, RetP.
ROW 116: 57 C, 20 E, 100 D, RetP.
ROW 117: 56 C, 22 E, 99 D, RetP.
ROW 118: 55 C, 24 E, 98 D, RetP.
ROW 119: 54 C, 26 E, 97 D, RetP.
ROW 120: 53 C, 28 E, 96 D, RetP.
ROW 121: 52 C, 30 E, 95 D, RetP.
ROW 122: 51 C, 32 E, 94 D, RetP.
ROW 123: 50 C, 34 E, 93 D, RetP.
ROW 124: 50 C, 35 E, 92 D, RetP.
ROW 125: 49 C, 36 E, 92 D, RetP.
ROW 126: 48 C, 38 E, 91 D, RetP.
ROW 127: 47 C, 40 E, 90 D, RetP.
ROW 128: 47 C, 41 E, 89 D, RetP.
ROW 129: 46 C, 43 E, 88 D, RetP.
ROW 130: 45 C, 45 E, 87 D, RetP.
ROW 131: 44 C, 47 E, 86 D, RetP.
ROW 132: 43 C, 49 E, 85 D, RetP.
ROW 133: 42 C, 51 E, 84 D, RetP.
ROW 134: 41 C, 54 E, 82 D, RetP.
ROW 135: 41 C, 55 E, 81 D, RetP.
ROW 136: 40 C, 57 E, 80 D, RetP.
ROW 137: 39 C, 59 E, 79 D, RetP.
ROW 138: 38 C, 61 E, 78 D, RetP.

ROW 139: 37 C, 63 E, 77 D, RetP.
ROW 140: 36 C, 65 E, 76 D, RetP.
ROW 141: 35 C, 67 E, 75 D, RetP.
ROW 142: 35 C, 68 E, 74 D, RetP.
ROW 143: 34 C, 71 E, 72 D, RetP.
ROW 144: 33 C, 73 E, 71 D, RetP.
ROW 145: 32 C, 75 E, 70 D, RetP.
ROW 146: 31 C, 77 E, 69 D, RetP.
ROW 147: 31 C, 78 E, 68 D, RetP.
ROW 148: 30 C, 80 E, 67 D, RetP.
ROW 149: 29 C, 82 E, 66 D, RetP.
ROW 150: 28 C, 84 E, 65 D, RetP.
ROW 151: 27 C, 86 E, 64 D, RetP.
ROW 152: 26 C, 88 E, 63 D, RetP.
ROW 153: 26 C, 90 E, 61 D, RetP.
ROW 154: 25 C, 92 E, 60 D, RetP.
ROW 155: 24 C, 94 E, 59 D, RetP.
ROW 156: 24 C, 95 E, 58 D, RetP.
ROW 157: 23 C, 97 E, 57 D, RetP.
ROW 158: 22 C, 99 E, 56 D, RetP.
ROW 159: 21 C, 101 E, 55 D, RetP.
ROW 160: 20 C, 103 E, 54 D, RetP.
ROW 161: 20 C, 104 E, 53 D, RetP.
ROW 162: 19 C, 106 E, 52 D, RetP.
ROW 163: 18 C, 109 E, 50 D, RetP.
ROW 164: 17 C, 111 E, 49 D, RetP.
ROW 165: 16 C, 113 E, 48 D, RetP.
ROW 166: 16 C, 114 E, 47 D, RetP.
ROW 167: 15 C, 116 E, 46 D, RetP.
ROW 168: 14 C, 118 E, 45 D, RetP.
ROW 169: 13 C, 120 E, 44 D, RetP.
ROW 170: 12 C, 122 E, 43 D, RetP.
ROW 171: 12 C, 123 E, 42 D, RetP.
ROW 172: 11 C, 125 E, 41 D, RetP.
ROW 173: 10 C, 127 E, 40 D, RetP.
ROW 174: 9 C, 129 E, 39 D, RetP.
ROW 175: 8 C, 132 E, 37 D, RetP.
ROW 176: 7 C, 134 E, 36 D, RetP.
Cc to F on last st of RetP. Remove Tunisian crochet hook.

BIND OFF AND BORDER

ROUND 1: With F and standard crochet hook, ch 1, *pull up a loop in the next vertical bar as for tss, yo, pull through both loops on hook (sc made), repeat from * across row, being sure to insert hook as for Lts on the last stitch, ch 2, working in row ends sc in each edge st to next corner, ch 2, working in unused lps of Row 1 foundation ch, sc in each ch across to next corner, ch 2, working in row ends sc in each edge st to next corner, ch 2, sl st in first sc of round.

ROUND 2: Ch 1, [sc in each sc to next ch-2 sp, (sc 1, ch 1, sc 1) in ch-2 sp] around, sl st in first sc of round.

ROUND 3: Ch 1, [sc in each sc to next ch-2 sp, (sc 1, ch 1, sc 1) in ch-2 sp] 4 times, sc in each remaining sc, sl st in first sc of round.
Fasten off.

FINISHING

Weave in any remaining ends and block to finished dimensions.

Lexington Cashmere Gloves

There's no fiber more sumptuously soft and touchable than small-batch 100 percent cashmere, which makes it the ideal pairing for these fingerless gloves. A timeless accessory like this is perfect for the modern lifestyle by keeping your digits free for texting and selfies.

Add some Parisian flair to your fall wardrobe with this quick project. These gloves are constructed using central increases to create thumb gussets with a flawless fit. Subtle ribbed edges offer durability and a tidy finish.

FINISHED SIZE
7¼" (18.5 cm) circumference × 7¼" (18.5 cm) long

YARN
Clinton Hill Cashmere Bespoke (100% Italian cashmere), category 4—heavy worsted/Aran weight, 99 yds (91 m)/50 g (1½ oz). *Color: Camel, 120 yds (110 m), (2 balls).*

HOOKS
Size US J/10 (6 mm) Tunisian crochet hook with 16-inch (40.5-cm) cord
Or size needed to obtain gauge
Size US H/8 (5 mm) crochet hook

NOTIONS
Stitch markers
Tapestry needle

GAUGE
15 sts and 12 rows = 4" (10 cm) with Tunisian crochet hook in Tunisian simple stitch, unblocked

STITCHES AND TECHNIQUES
- Tunisian simple stitch
- Single crochet in back loop only
- Picking up stitches
- Increasing in the back bar
- Whipstitch seam
- Mattress stitch seam

NOTE
Increase (*inc*) means to pull up a loop in the back bar of the next stitch (stitch count increased by +1).

GLOVE (MAKE 2)

RIBBING

ROW 1: With standard crochet hook, ch 6, sc in 2nd ch from hook and each st across row, turn. (5 sc)

ROW 2: Ch 1, sc BLO across row, turn.

ROWS 3-23: Rep Row 2. Rotate ribbing to work along row ends.

HAND

ROW 1: With Tunisian crochet hook, sk first row, pull up a loop in the end of each remaining row across ribbing (**Photo 1**), RetP. (23 tss)

ROW 2: Tss 1, inc, tss 19, inc, tss 1, Lts, RetP. (25 tss)

ROW 3: Tss across row to last st, Lts, RetP.

ROW 4: Tss 1, inc, tss 21, inc, tss 1, Lts, RetP. (27 tss)

ROWS 5-6: Rep Row 3.

ROW 7: Tss 12, inc, tss 1, inc, tss 12, Lts, RetP. (29 tss)

ROW 8: Tss 12, inc, tss 3, inc, tss 12, Lts, RetP. (31 tss)

ROW 9: Tss 12, inc, tss 5, inc, tss 12, Lts, RetP. (33 tss)

ROW 10: Tss 12, inc, tss 7, inc, tss 12, Lts, RetP. (35 tss)

ROW 11: Tss 12, inc, tss 9, inc, tss 12, Lts, RetP. (37 tss)
Place marker in live loop. Do not cut yarn.

THUMB

ROW 1: Sk 14 sts, with opposite end of yarn ball and Tunisian hook, pull up a loop in each of the next 9 sts (**Photo 2**), RetP. (9 tss)

ROW 2: Tss across row to last st, Lts, RetP. Sl st bind off loosely. Do not fasten off.

THUMB RIBBING

ROW 1: With standard crochet hook, ch 4, sc in 2nd ch from hook and each of next 2 chs, sl st in thumb st at base of ch and next sl st on thumb bind-off edge, turn. (3 sc)

ROW 2: Sk 2 sl sts, sc BLO across row, turn. (3 sc)

ROW 3: Ch 1, sc BLO in each sc, sl st in next 2 sts on bind-off edge, turn.

ROWS 4-7: Rep Rows 2 and 3.

ROW 8: Rep Row 2.

ROW 9: Ch 1, sc BLO in each sc, sl st in last sl st on thumb bind-off edge.
Fasten off leaving a long tail for seaming.

HAND, CONT'D

ROW 12: Remove marker, replace loop on Tunisian hook. With Tunisian hook, tss 13, sk thumb sts, tss 13 in remaining sts of hand, Lts, RetP. (28 tss)

ROWS 13-16: Tss across row to last st, Lts, RetP. Sl st bind off loosely after last row.

1. Picking up loops in ribbing row end

2. Skipping stitches to work thumb

HAND RIBBING

With standard crochet hook, ch 4, sc in 2nd ch from hook and each of next 2 chs, sl st in st at base of ch and next sl st on bind-off edge, turn. (3 sc)

Repeat Rows 2 and 3 from Thumb Ribbing across edge, ending with a Row 2 repeat. Do not turn after last row. Fasten off, leaving a long tail for seaming.

FINISHING

Pin glove flat with RS facing up and steam block lightly. This step gives the glove some flexibility. Do not stretch the hand or the ribbing.

Use the tail from the thumb to whipstitch seam the sides of the thumb together, being sure to close any hole left at the base of the thumb.

Use tail to mattress seam sides of glove together.

Weave in all remaining ends.

Keyhole Hanging Planter

Show of hands—where are all of my houseplant parents?!
These hanging planters transform store-bought canning jars
into containers that are just right for your most prized plants
and vines.

Worked using a combination of traditional and Tunisian crochet,
the keyhole accent lets you keep an eye on each plant's soil and
roots. You can get three planters out of one ball of yarn, making
it easy to swap out colors as your decor changes with several
planters leftover to gift to friends and neighbors.

FINISHED SIZE
11½" (29 cm) circumference ×
4" (10 cm) height × 16" (40.5 cm)
long strap

YARN
Lion Brand Rewind (70%
polyester, 30% viscose),
category 5—bulky weight, 219 yds
(200 m)/100 g (3½ oz). *Colors:
Sample 1 in #159 Citronella and
Sample 2 in #123 Greige, 68 yds
(63 m) each, (1 skein each).*

HOOKS
Size US H/8 (5 mm) crochet hook
Or size needed to obtain gauge
Size US I/9 (5.5 mm) Tunisian
crochet hook with 16-inch
(40.5-cm) cord

NOTIONS
Two 10-mm wooden beads
16-ounce wide-mouth glass
canning jar
Stitch markers
Tapestry needle

GAUGE
Finished base measures 5"
(13 cm) in diameter when made
with 5 mm crochet hook and
pressed flat.

STITCHES AND TECHNIQUES
• Magic ring
• Single crochet in a spiral
• Single crochet in back loop only
• Single crochet in joined rounds
• Tunisian arrowhead stitch

NOTES

- Use a locking stitch marker to mark your rounds when working the flat rounds of the Base and the Side, Round 1.
- Convert the hanging planter into a traditional planter cover by omitting the strap.
- Don't like the keyhole accent? Use a length of yarn to whip-stitch seam the keyhole closed.

DIRECTIONS

BASE

ROUND 1: With standard crochet hook, make MR, ch 1, sc 6 in ring, pull tail to close ring, do not join, continue to work in a spiral. (6 sts)

ROUND 2: 2 sc in each st around. (12 sts)

ROUND 3: (2 sc in next st, sc in next st) around. (18 sts)

ROUND 4: Sc in next st, (2 sc in next st, sc in next 2 sts) 5 times, 2 sc in next st, sc in last st. (24 sts)

ROUND 5: (2 sc in next st, sc in next 3 sts) around. (30 sts)

ROUND 6: Sc in next 3 sts, (2 sc in next st, sc in next 4 sts) 5 times, 2 sc in next st, sc in last st. (36 sts)

SIDE

ROUND 1: Sc BLO in each st around.

ROUND 2: Sl st in next st, ch 1, sc in same st and each st around, join with a sl st in the first sc of the round.

ROUND 3: Ch 1, sc in same st as join and each st around, join with a sl st in the first sc of the round. Remove standard crochet hook.

ROW 4: With Tunisian crochet hook, pull up a loop in the next st and each st around, RetP. (36 sts) **(Photo 1)**

ROW 5: (Tss2tog, yo) to last st, Lts, RetP.

ROW 6: (Tss the next st, tks the yo) to last st, Lts, RetP.

ROWS 7-12: Rep Rows 2 and 3 three times. Drop Tunisian crochet hook at the end of the RetP of the last row.

ROUND 13: With standard crochet hook, ch 1, sc in the vertical bar of the first st and each st around, join with a sl st in the first sc of the round. Use a locking stitch marker to mark the 9th and 27th stitches of this round. (36 sts) **(Photos 2 and 3)**

ROUND 14: Ch 1, sc in same st as join and each st around, join with a sl st in the first sc of the round. Fasten off and weave in all ends.

1. Pulling up loops in Row 4

2. Single crochet after Tunisian section with join

3. Placing stitch markers

4. Adding the tails through the marked stitches

STRAP

ROW 1: With standard crochet hook and leaving a 10" (25-cm) tail, ch until piece measures 16" (40.5 cm) length when slightly stretched. Fasten off leaving a 10" (25-cm) tail.

ROW 2: Leaving a 10" (25-cm) tail and working in the back bumps of the chain, join with a sl st in the last ch from Row 1, sl st in each ch across row. Fasten off leaving a 10" (25-cm) tail.

ASSEMBLY AND FINISHING

Thread one wooden bead onto both tails at one end of the strap. Thread one tail through one of the marked stitches from Round 13. Securely knot the tails together and weave in ends. Repeat this step for the other end of the strap. (**Photos 4 and 5**)

Measure 2" (5 cm) down from the middle of the strap. Wrap a length of yarn around both thicknesses of the strap multiple times to create a loop. Weave ends into the strap. Insert the canning jar into the planter.

5. Weaving in strap end

Pemba Cardi

The classic chunky cardigan is a maker wardrobe must-have. This design is simple enough to be your first sweater project: The honeycomb pattern is easy to memorize while the oversize silhouette requires minimal shaping. Extra-thick ribbed bands around the edges give this piece a polished yet casual look.

Need some outfit ideas? Pair this cardigan with a crisp shirtdress or a beloved concert tee and distressed denim. Afternoon errands or weekend brunch—wherever you go in this cardi, you'll be going in style.

FINISHED SIZES
S/M (L/XL, 2XL/3XL)

FINISHED SIZE
Bust: 54 (60, 66)" [137 (152.5, 167.5) cm]
Length: 29 (30, 31)" [74 (76, 79) cm]

YARN
Universal Yarn Deluxe Bulky (100% superwash wool), category 5—bulky weight, 106 yds (97 m)/100 g (3½ oz).
Color: #932 Icy Grey, 1325 (1530, 1745) yds [1211.5 (1399, 1596) m], [13 (15, 17) balls].

HOOKS
Size US L/11 (8 mm) crochet hook
Size US N/15 (10 mm) Tunisian crochet hook with 24-inch (61-cm) cord
Or size needed to obtain gauge
Size 7 mm crochet hook

NOTIONS
Stitch markers
Tapestry needle

GAUGE
16 sts and 12 rows = 6" (15 cm) with Tunisian crochet hook in pattern stitch, unblocked

STITCHES AND TECHNIQUES
- Honeycomb stitch
- Single crochet in back loop only
- Picking up stitches
- Increasing in the back bar
- Mattress stitch seam
- Applied ribbing technique

- This pattern is created in separate pieces, then seamed together: one Back panel, two Front panels, and two Sleeves.
- Increase (abbreviated *inc*) means to pull up a loop in the back bar of the next stitch (stitch count increased by +1).
- Pattern is written for S/M size with additional sizes in parentheses. For some sections, instructions for the different sizes are written separately. Only follow instructions for the size you are making.
- Adjust the width of the cardigan by crocheting more or less ribbing rows. Complete the ribbing to an even number of rows. Adjust the length of the cardigan by crocheting more or less rows after the ribbing.
- Find on page 46 a photo tutorial of the applied ribbing technique used in the Neckline Ribbing section.

DIRECTIONS

BACK

LOWER RIBBING

ROW 1: With US L/11 (8 mm) hook, ch 9, sc in the 2nd ch from hook and each ch across, turn. (8 sc)

ROW 2: Ch 1, sc BLO across row, turn.

Repeat Row 2 to 72 (80, 88) total rows.

Rotate ribbing to work along row ends.

BACK BODY

ROW 1: With Tunisian crochet hook, sk first row, pull up a loop in the end of each remaining row across ribbing (**Photo 1**), RetP. [72 (80, 88) sts]

ROW 2: (Tss 1, tps 1) across row to last st, Lts, RetP.

ROW 3: (Tps 1, tss 1) across row to last st, Lts, RetP.

Repeat Rows 2 and 3 to 54 (56, 58) total rows. Sl st bind off loosely after last row. Fasten off.

1. Pulling up loops along ribbing row edge

FRONT (MAKE 2)

LOWER RIBBING

ROW 1: With US L/11 (8 mm) hook, ch 9, sc in the 2nd ch from hook and each ch across, turn. (8 sc)

ROW 2: Ch 1, sc BLO across row, turn.

Repeat Row 2 to 24 (26, 28) total rows.

Rotate ribbing to work along row ends.

FRONT BODY

ROW 1: With Tunisian crochet hook, sk first row, pull up a loop in the end of each remaining row across ribbing, RetP. [24 (26, 28) sts]

ROW 2: (Tss 1, tps 1) across row to last st, Lts, RetP.

ROW 3: (Tps 1, tss 1) across row to last st, Lts, RetP.

Repeat Rows 2 and 3 to 54 (56, 58) total rows. Sl st bind off loosely after last row. Fasten off.

SLEEVE (MAKE 2)

LOWER RIBBING

ROW 1: With 7 mm hook, ch 9, sc in the 2nd ch from hook and each ch across, turn. (8 sc)

ROW 2: Ch 1, sc BLO across row, turn.

Repeat Row 2 to 18 (20, 22) total rows.

Rotate ribbing to work along row ends.

SLEEVE, SIZE S/M ONLY

ROW 1: With Tunisian crochet hook, sk first row, pull up a loop in the end of each remaining row across ribbing, RetP. (18 sts)

ROW 2: [(Tss 1, inc) 3 times, tss 1] 4 times, Lts, RetP. (30 sts)

ROW 3: [Tss 4, (tss 1, inc) 3 times] 4 times, Lts, RetP. (42 sts)

ROW 4: (Tss 1, tps 1) across row to last st, Lts, RetP.

ROW 5: (Tps 1, tss 1) across row to last st, Lts, RetP.

ROWS 6-31: Repeat Rows 4 and 5. Sl st bind off loosely after last row. Fasten off, leaving a long tail for seaming.

SLEEVE, SIZE L/XL ONLY

ROW 1: With Tunisian crochet hook, sk first row, pull up a loop in the end of each remaining row across ribbing, RetP. (20 sts)

ROW 2: [(Tss 1, inc) 4 times, tss 1] 3 times, (tss 1, inc) 3 times, Lts, RetP. (35 sts)

ROW 3: [Tss 3, (tss 1, inc) 2 times] 6 times, (tss 1, inc) 3 times, Lts, RetP. (50 sts)

ROW 4: (Tss 1, tps 1) across row to last st, Lts, RetP.

ROW 5: (Tps 1, tss 1) across row to last st, Lts, RetP.

ROWS 6-31: Repeat Rows 4 and 5. Sl st bind off loosely after last row. Fasten off, leaving a long tail for seaming.

SLEEVE, SIZE 2XL/3XL ONLY

ROW 1: With Tunisian crochet hook, sk first row, pull up a loop in the end of each remaining row across ribbing, RetP. (22 sts)

ROW 2: [(Tss 1, inc) 3 times, tss 1] 5 times, Lts, RetP. (37 sts)

ROW 3: [Tss 3, (tss 1, inc) 2 times] 6 times, tss 2, (tss 1, inc) 3 times, Lts, RetP. (52 sts)

ROW 4: (Tss 1, tps 1) across row to last st, Lts, RetP.

ROW 5: (Tps 1, tss 1) across row to last st, Lts, RetP.

ROWS 6-31: Repeat Rows 4 and 5. Sl st bind off loosely after last row. Fasten off, leaving a long tail for seaming.

ASSEMBLY

Hold Back and one Front panel together with RS facing out. Use leftover tail from Front to mattress seam the shoulder, working one stitch on Front to one stitch on Back. Weave in end. Repeat for the other Front panel. After seaming, there should be a 9 (10½, 12)-inch [23 (26.5, 30.5)-cm] space between the Front panels for the neck opening.

Block sleeve with width at bind-off edge at 16 (18½, 20)" [40.5 (47, 51) cm]. Lay seamed Body and Fronts flat with RS facing up. Use locking stitch markers to line up one Sleeve with the Body. Align the midpoint of the sleeve with the shoulder seam. Mattress seam the Sleeve to the Body. Weave in end. Repeat for the other Sleeve. Fold cardigan in half. Use a length of yarn to mattress seam the sides, beginning at the Sleeve Ribbing, working toward the underarm and down the side of the cardigan. Weave in the remaining ends. Repeat for the other side.

NECKLINE RIBBING

ROW 1: With US L/11 (8 mm) hook, sl st to join in the bottom corner of the ribbing on the right Front panel. Ch 9, sc in 2nd ch from hook and each ch across row, sl st in the same st as join, sl st in the next st on the Front panel, turn. (**Photos 2–4**)

ROW 2: Sk 2 sl sts, sc BLO across row, turn.

ROW 3: Ch 1, sc BLO across row, sl st in next 2 sts on the Front panel, turn.

Rep Rows 2 and 3 up the front panel. As you work upwards, you will be working sl sts into row ends on the Front panel. Continue to repeat Rows 2 and 3 across the neck opening and down the other Front panel. When complete, fasten off.

FINISHING

Weave in any remaining ends and block to finished dimensions.

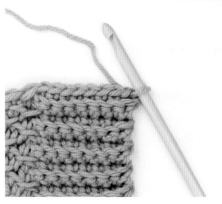

2. Joining in bottom corner of right Front panel ribbing

3. Sc in each ch

4. First 4 rows of neckline ribbing

Hazelwood Lattice Pillow

That lattice look is a fresh way to update your home decor. Plus, it's really fun to see this piece come together as you're making it. Worked in a squishy alpaca/merino-blend yarn, the woven stripes make a double-thick fabric that's extra plush. The contrasting backing adds an unexpected pop of color.

Whether you're sinking into a cup of tea and a book or cuddling up to binge your favorite series, this is soon to be your favorite pillow on the couch.

FINISHED SIZE
18" (46 cm) square

YARN
WeCrochet City Tweed Aran (55% merino wool, 25% superfine alpaca, 20% Donegal tweed), category 4—heavy worsted/Aran weight, 164 yds (150 m)/100 g (3½ oz). *Colors: (A) Snowshoe, (B) Orca, (C) Romance, 190 yds (173 m) each, (2 balls each).*

HOOK
Size US K/10½ (6.5 mm) Tunisian crochet hook with 16-inch (40.5-cm) cord
Or size needed to obtain gauge

NOTIONS
18-inch (46-cm) square pillow form
Stitch markers
Tapestry needle

GAUGE
13 sts and 10 rows = 4" (10 cm) in Tunisian simple stitch, unblocked

STITCHES AND TECHNIQUES
• Tunisian simple stitch
• Whipstitch seam

DIRECTIONS

FRONT

STRIP 1

ROW 1: With A, ch 58, pull up a loop in the 2nd ch from hook and each ch across row, RetP. (58 sts)

ROW 2: Tss across row to last st, Lts, RetP.

ROWS 3-7: Rep Row 2.

Sl st bind off loosely after last row. Use instructions from Strip 1 to make six total strips in A and six total strips in B. Weave in all ends. Block strips to 17" (43 cm) long × 2¾" (7 cm) wide.

Weave strips into lattice pattern using locking stitch markers on the ends to hold strips in place. Set aside. **(Photo 1)**

BACK

ROW 1: With C, ch 58, pull up a loop in the 2nd ch from hook and each ch across row, RetP. (58 sts)

ROW 2: Tss across row to last st, Lts, RetP.

ROWS 3-46: Rep Row 2.

Sl st bind off loosely after last row. Steam block Back to 17¾" (45 cm) × 17¾" (45 cm).

ASSEMBLY AND FINISHING

Lay Front and Back together with WS facing each other. Use a strand of C to whipstitch seam three sides of the square together, working through all three thicknesses of fabric and removing stitch markers as you go.

Insert the pillow form. Whipstitch the remaining side of the pillow closed.

To close gaps in the lattice on the Front, use B to whipstitch 1-2 stitches closed on each side of every color A strip. **(Photo 2)** Weave in any remaining ends.

1. Lattice pattern of strips

2. Seaming strip gaps closed

Pinwheel Pet Bed

Our furry friends seem to love sleeping on top of our projects, am I right? Give your pup or kitty their very own handmade masterpiece with this darling lounge.

The choice of an acrylic/wool-blend yarn makes this bed warm yet washable and offers lots of colors to choose from. The size can be easily adjusted—just start with a longer or shorter starting chain and adjust the yarn amounts accordingly. Removable plastic mesh canvas panels reinforce the sides.

FINISHED SIZE
18" (46 cm) diameter × 4" (10 cm) tall

YARN
Berroco Vintage Chunky (52% acrylic, 40% wool, 8% nylon), category 5—bulky weight, 136 yds (124 m)/100 g (3½ oz). *Colors: (A) #6106 Smoke, 230 yds (210 m), (2 skeins); (B) #6109 Storm, 265 yds (242 m), (2 skeins).*

HOOKS
Size US K/10½ (6.5 mm) Tunisian crochet hook with 16-inch (40.5-cm) cord
Size US K/10½ (6.5 mm) double-ended Tunisian crochet hook
Or size needed to obtain gauge

NOTIONS
Two clear #7 mesh plastic canvas sheets measuring 10½" (26.5 cm) × 13½" (34 cm)
Stitch marker
Tapestry needle

GAUGE
14 sts and 12 rows = 4" (10 cm) in Tunisian simple stitch, unblocked

STITCHES AND TECHNIQUES
• Tunisian simple stitch
• Short row increases
• Mattress stitch seam
• Tunisian crochet in the round
• Changing colors (stripes)

NOTES
• Make your pet bed larger or smaller by adjusting the number of stitches in your starting chain. Be sure the stitch count is a multiple of two.
• The last stitch of all wedges is worked into the marked stitch from the original chain. This will ensure that you do not have a hole in the center of your work.
• Remove the plastic canvas before laundering.

SECOND WEDGE

ROW 1: Tss next st, ch 1, yo, pull through both loops on hook. (2 sts)

ROW 2: Tss next st, tss next unworked st on the last row of the first wedge, RetP. (3 sts)

ROW 3: Tss next 2 sts, tss next unworked st on the last row of the first wedge, RetP. (4 sts)

ROWS 4-26: Continue as for Row 3 by picking up one new stitch on the last row of the previous wedge on the forward pass until you have worked 27 stitches from the first wedge. (27 sts)

ROW 27: Tss next st and each st across until 27 loops on hook, sk the last st, pull up a loop in the marked chain (**Photo 1**), RetP, cc to A when 2 loops remain on hook. Fasten off B. (28 sts)
Continuing with A, repeat instructions from the second wedge, alternating wedge colors, until you have 6 total wedges. Do not change color after the last wedge. Sl st bind off loosely. Fasten off leaving a long tail for seaming.

DIRECTIONS

BASE

FIRST WEDGE

ROW 1: With corded Tunisian crochet hook and A, ch 28. Place a locking stitch marker in the first ch made. Pull up a loop in the back bump of the 2nd ch from hook, ch 1, yo, pull through both loops on hook. (2 sts)

ROW 2: Tss next st, pull up a loop in the back bump of the next ch, RetP. (3 sts)

ROW 3: Tss next 2 sts, pull up a loop in the back bump of the next ch, RetP. (4 sts)
Continue as for Row 3 by picking up one new stitch in the next foundation chain on the forward pass of each row until you have worked into each of the 28 foundation chains. On the last RetP, cc to B when 2 loops remain on the hook. Fasten off A.

1. Pulling up a loop in the marked stitch on wedge

ROUNDS 14–24: Continue working tss in the round. On last round, complete RetP until 1 loop is left on hook. Position hook as for FwdP in the round. Sl st bind off loosely. Fasten off B.

FINISHING

Weave in any remaining ends. Cut four 4" (10 cm) × 13½" (34 cm) strips of plastic canvas. Place strips inside pet bed along the bottom half of sides, slightly overlapping them to reinforce the sides. Fold the top half of the side over the plastic canvas.

Steam block side and base lightly as needed.

Optional: Use B to whipstitch seam the bind-off edge to the base of the bed. This will create a cleaner look to the bed but will cause it to no longer be machine washable.

Remove marker. Use the remaining tail to mattress seam the bind-off row to starting chain stitches. Weave in all ends. Steam block lightly to 18" (46 cm) diameter.

SIDE

ROUND 1: With double-ended Tunisian crochet hook and A, with WS facing, pull up a loop in each st around base edge. (**Photo 2**) Begin working tss in the round, completing the RetP in the same color using a separate ball of yarn. Place a stitch marker on the first stitch of the round and move the marker up in subsequent rounds.

ROUND 2–12: Continue working tss in the round.

ROUND 13: Cc to B by pulling up a loop in B in the first st of the FwdP of this round. Continue working tss in the round, changing to B on the RetP when 1 loop of A remains. Fasten off A.

2. Picking up stitches along the base edge

Bliss Braided Ear Warmer

An ear warmer can hide a bad hair day or keep your ears protected without giving you hat head. But what if you could marry form and function?

This braided version elevates the classic accessory to a radiant crown, letting you show off the gorgeous single-ply roving yarn with a luxe but simple Tunisian stitch. The braided technique is fun to do and makes the piece look way more complicated than it is. (Did someone say Secret Santa?!)

FINISHED SIZE
4½" (10 cm) wide × 20" (51 cm) long after braiding; sized to fit head circumference 20-22" (51-56 cm)

YARN
Kenyarn Cumulus (80% superwash merino, 20% nylon), category 5—bulky weight, 76 yds (69.5 m)/100 g (3½ oz). *Colors: Sample 1 in Peanut and Sample 2 in Sheba, 100 yds (91.5 m) each, (2 skeins each).*

HOOK
Size US K/10½ (6.5 mm) Tunisian crochet hook
Or size needed to obtain gauge

NOTIONS
Clipboard or other mechanism to hold ear warmer when braiding
Stitch marker

GAUGE
4" (10 cm) = 14 stitches × 10 rows in Tunisian simple stitch, unblocked

STITCHES AND TECHNIQUES
• Tunisian simple stitch
• Mattress stitch seam

DIRECTIONS

FOUNDATION

Ch 16, pull up a loop in the 2nd ch from hook and each ch across row, RetP.

STRIP 1

ROW 1: Tss next 3 sts, leave remaining stitches unworked (**Photo 1**), RetP. (4 sts)

ROW 2: Tss across row to last st, Lts, RetP. (4 sts)

ROWS 3–61: Repeat Row 2. Strip 1 should measure 25½" (65 cm) from Foundation to working row. Drop the hook. Secure the live loop with a locking stitch marker. Cut the yarn leaving a 3" (7.5-cm) tail.

STRIP 2

ROW 1: Pull up a loop in each of the next 4 sts from Foundation (**Photo 2**), RetP. (4 sts)

ROW 2: Tss across row to last st, Lts, RetP.

ROWS 3–61: Repeat Row 2. Strip should measure 25½" (65 cm) from Foundation to working row. Drop the hook. Secure the live loop with a locking stitch marker. Cut the yarn leaving a 3" (7.5-cm) tail.

STRIPS 3 AND 4

Repeat instructions from Strip 2.

BRAIDING

Optional: The strips will be easier to braid when they are relaxed. Pin piece to a blocking board and steam block lightly to relax the strips. Let the piece dry completely before braiding.

Secure the Foundation row to a clipboard so Strip 1 is on the left, followed by Strips 2 and 3, with Strip 4 at the right edge.

Braid the ear warmer using the following sequence (**Photos 3 and 4**):

• Step 1: Cross 1 over 2.
• Step 2: Cross 3 over 4.
• Step 3: Cross 4 over 1.

After working steps 1–3, the strip on the left edge is now 1, followed (from left to right) by 2, 3, and 4. Repeat the braid steps sequence as many times as you can, securing the final braid with locking stitch markers. (**Photo 5**)

Remove the ear warmer from the clipboard and position the piece to begin crocheting along the ends of the strips.

NEXT ROW: Remove the marker from the live loop of the strip farthest to the right. Place the loop on the hook. Using yarn from the ball (not from the tails of the piece), pull up a loop in the remaining 3 sts of the strip. (Remove marker from the next strip's live loop, place live loop on hook, pull up a loop in each of the remaining 3 sts of the strip) for each of the remaining strips, RetP. (**Photo 6**)

Sl st bind off, leaving a long tail for seaming. Fasten off.

FINISHING

With right sides facing up, bring ends of the ear warmer together and join with a mattress seam using the remaining tail.

Weave in any remaining ends.

1. First 4 loops of Strip 1

2. First 4 loops of Strip 2

3. Braiding (1 over 2 and 3 over 4)

4. Braiding (4 over 1)

5. Finished braid with locking stitch markers

6. Forward pass over live loops

Resources

My unending gratitude goes out to every company that provided yarn support for this book. From the established corporations to the independent dyers and everyone in between, thank you for giving so generously to my project.

Berroco
berroco.com

Clinton Hill Cashmere
clintonhillcashmere.com

Kenyarn
kenyarn.com

Lion Brand Yarns
lionbrand.com

LoveCrafts
lovecrafts.com

Madelinetosh
madelinetosh.com

Malabrigo
malabrigoyarn.com

Universal Yarn
universalyarn.com

We Are Knitters
weareknitters.com

WeCrochet
crochet.com

Yarnspirations
yarnspirations.com

Kudos

The Tunisian Crochet Handbook would still be on my bucket list if it weren't for that initial e-mail from **Abrams**. Special thanks go to **Meredith** for seeing my potential and helping me hone my vision. I'm so grateful for the opportunity.

To **Stefanie** and the team at **Full Circle Literary**, thank you for teaching me the business, advocating on my behalf, and always having an encouraging word.

An especially grateful thanks goes to you, **Emily** and **Janine**, for weeding through my notes and helping me achieve a polished product. I know readers and makers will appreciate your diligence. To my new friend **Christina**, thank you for adding flair and personality to my pieces, endearing me to each one even more. And to my beautiful and talented friends **Ashley**, **Britt**, **Janine**, **Kasey**, **Nkese**, **Siobhan**, and **Stacie**—I love you all so much—for lending me your talent as pattern testers and keeping the jokes coming long after testing was done.

When I say "I don't know where I would be without you," I sincerely mean it, **Jenon**. You quell my doubts at every turn. You consistently encourage me to reach for new heights that I've never dreamed of. Thank you for keeping me fed and caffeinated for these many months. I owe you at least five pots of macaroni and cheese.

I don't think I have enough words in my vocabulary to thank you, **Edward** and **Gwendolyn**. As my parents, I know that your love and support are what have buoyed me to the place I find myself in now. Thank you, Dad, for your silly jokes and thoughtful advice. Thank you, Mom, for laughing with me and showing me that I should never hide my strength.

To **Auntie Ife** and **Cousin Myette**, thank you for continuing the legacy of crochet and craft in our family.

They say a picture is worth a thousand words. I knew from the very start that **Allie** and **The Wonder Jam** would know exactly how to tell my story, and I was not disappointed. Thank you for understanding the exact things I didn't know how to say. To **Sha'ra** and **Jeannine**, thank you for bringing my creations to life. I can't wait to fake laugh at our shoulders together again soon. And thank you, **Sergio**, for opening your home to me for this project. **The Jungle** provided the perfect backdrop for the journey of this book.

So many friends lent their ears and their wisdom to me while I was writing *The Tunisian Crochet Handbook*. Thank you to **Alexi** and **Teresa**, for the grilled cheeses, the laughs, and reminding me that I'm not in this alone. To **Jake**, who always seems to text me right when I need a break the most: I can't wait for our PCCB date. To **Rohn, Lee**, and **Vincent,** my crafty mentors who have taught me so much and proved that anything is possible. And to my OPKs **Crystal, Annelisa**, and **Courtney**. I wouldn't be who I am without my best friends. I love you so much.

My final and most gracious thanks go to you, the person reading this book. Thank you for trusting a portion of your maker experience with me. You are part of the TLYC Makers family now, and I can't wait to see what you create.

Editor: Meredith A. Clark
Designer: Darilyn Lowe Carnes with Shawn Dahl
Production Manager: Anet Sirna-Bruder

Library of Congress Control Number: 2021932575

ISBN: 978-1-4197-4718-2
eISBN: 978-1-68335-994-4

Printed and bound in China
9 10 8

Abrams books are available at special discounts when purchased in quantity for premiums and promotions as well as fundraising or educational use. Special editions can also be created to specification. For details, contact specialsales@abramsbooks.com or the address below.

Abrams® is a registered trademark of Harry N. Abrams, Inc.

ABRAMS The Art of Books
195 Broadway, New York, NY 10007
abramsbooks.com